NEW DIRECTIONS FOR CHILD AND ADOLESCENT DEVELOPMENT

William Damon, *Stanford University*
EDITOR-IN-CHIEF

Symbolic and Social Constraints on the Development of Children's Artistic Style

Chris J. Boyatzis
Bucknell University

Malcolm W. Watson
Brandeis University

EDITORS

Number 90, Winter 2000

JOSSEY-BASS
San Francisco

SYMBOLIC AND SOCIAL CONSTRAINTS ON THE DEVELOPMENT OF CHILDREN'S
ARTISTIC STYLE
Chris J. Boyatzis, Malcolm W. Watson (eds.)
New Directions for Child and Adolescent Development, no. 90
William Damon, Editor-in-Chief

© 2000 by Jossey-Bass Inc. All rights reserved.

Jossey-Bass is a registered trademark of Jossey-Bass Inc., A Wiley Company.

No part of this publication may be reproduced, stored in a retrieval system, or transmitted in any form or by any means, electronic, mechanical, photocopying, recording, scanning, or otherwise, except as permitted under Sections 107 or 108 of the 1976 United States Copyright Act, without either the prior written permission of the Publisher or authorization through payment of the appropriate per-copy fee to the Copyright Clearance Center, 222 Rosewood Drive, Danvers, MA 01923, (978) 750-8400, fax (978) 750-4744. Requests to the Publisher for permission should be addressed to the Permissions Department, John Wiley & Sons, Inc., 605 Third Avenue, New York, NY 10158-0012, (212) 850-6011, fax (212) 850-6008, e-mail: permreq@wiley.com.

Microfilm copies of issues and articles are available in 16mm and 35mm, as well as microfiche in 105mm, through University Microfilms Inc., 300 North Zeeb Road, Ann Arbor, MI 48106.

ISSN 1520-3247   ISBN 0-7879-1257-3

NEW DIRECTIONS FOR CHILD AND ADOLESCENT DEVELOPMENT is part of The Jossey-Bass Education Series and is published quarterly by Jossey-Bass Inc., 350 Sansome Street, San Francisco, CA 94104. Periodicals postage paid at San Francisco, California, and at additional mailing offices. Postmaster: Send address changes to New Directions for Child and Adolescent Development, Jossey-Bass Inc., 350 Sansome Street, San Francisco, CA 94104.

New Directions for Child and Adolescent Development is indexed in Biosciences Information Service, Current Index to Journals in Education (ERIC), Psychological Abstracts, and Sociological Abstracts.

SUBSCRIPTIONS cost $68.00 for individuals and $125.00 for institutions, agencies, and libraries.

EDITORIAL CORRESPONDENCE should be sent to the Editor-in-Chief, William Damon, Stanford Center on Adolescence, Cypress Building C, Stanford University, Stanford, CA 94305.

Cover photograph by Wernher Krutein/PHOTOVAULT © 1990.

Jossey-Bass Web address: www.josseybass.com

Printed in the United States of America on acid-free recycled paper containing 100 percent recovered waste paper, of which at least 20 percent is postconsumer waste.

Contents

Editors' Notes
Chris J. Boyatzis, Malcolm W. Watson — 1

1. **The Artistic Evolution of Mommy: A Longitudinal Case Study of Symbolic and Social Processes** — 5
Chris J. Boyatzis
A longitudinal case study of one girl's artistic development illustrates the interplay between the child's symbolic development and the social context in which the child draws. The observer-researcher can function as a "co-constructor" of artistic development, which highlights the need for models of development that integrate the constructs of a zone of proximal development, range of developmental level, and repertoire of skill.

2. **A Naturalistic Observation of Children Drawing: Peer Collaboration Processes and Influences in Children's Art** — 31
Chris J. Boyatzis, Gretchen Albertini
During the school years, boys and girls draw in strikingly different styles in content, technical quality, and meaning. In their group drawing sessions, fifth-grade boys and girls demonstrated an unrelenting commitment to realism in their art and displayed sociocognitive collaborative processes that could influence each other's artistic styles.

3. **The Development of Individual Styles in Children's Drawing** — 49
Malcolm W. Watson, Susan Nozyce Schwartz
When do individual styles emerge in children's art? And how do we know a style when we see it? Judges' analyses of three- to ten-year-olds' art reveal that a minority of children have a distinctive style that is apparent as early as the preschool years.

4. **Continuity of Styles in the Drawings of Adolescent Girls** — 65
Deborah J. Laible, Malcolm W. Watson, Elissa Koff
A longitudinal study of girls entering adolescence assessed the components of art that judges used to identify individual style. Distinctive style in girls' drawings was discernible over time but not across the time span when girls experienced menarche, suggesting that a girl's first menstrual period affects her art and disrupts her artistic style.

5. Looking for the Development of Artistic Style 81
in Children's Artworlds
Peter B. Pufall, Tuuli Pesonen
The components of artistic style were measured in longitudinal studies of young children. Innovative designs were used, including a retrospective measure in which judges used children's later drawings to identify their art from earlier in childhood. The concept of "artworld" helps elucidate children's art and style by accounting for the *how* and the *what* of children's art.

INDEX 99

Editors' Notes

The chapters in this volume address several important issues, but a central concern throughout is how scholars should conceptualize artistic development. Several chapters address more specifically the nature of artistic style.

Chapter One provides an introduction to symbolic and social processes in early artistic development. Chapter Two addresses the issue of style more directly, showing that style is gender-related and seems to be constrained by peers. The last three chapters are systematic studies of components of style and the developmental trajectory of style. The chapters address these questions: Do children have a discernible artistic style? What features of art do judges use to identify style? Does style change over childhood and adolescence? If so, what developments in other domains may influence stylistic change in art?

In Chapter One, Boyatzis presents a longitudinal case study of one child—the author's stepdaughter. The author describes sequences and processes of artistic development and emphasizes the interplay between endogenous symbolic processes within the child and social processes around the child. A theoretical significance of the chapter is the emphasis on the observer-researcher as an "art collaborator" or "co-constructor" of the child's art. The author also discusses complexities inherent in a stage model of artistic development. Werner's orthogenetic principle provides an organizing framework that can guide our understanding of the symbolic development in art. Clearly, the child's symbolic expression undergoes increasing differentiation and integration. But any endogenous change in the child might be understood within a zone of proximal development model that recognizes the co-construction of art between child and close observer (Vygotsky, 1978). As Fischer and Bidell (1998) describe in their "range of skill" model, skill is *in media res,* that is, in between the child and the context. Wolf's idea of a "repertoire" model of development (1994) illuminates the diversity and choice in symbolic expression and sheds light on the interplay between symbolic development and the social context's contributions to artistic growth.

In Chapter Two, Boyatzis and Albertini offer a descriptive observation of group drawing sessions in a fifth-grade classroom. After segregating themselves by gender, children began to draw. Two qualities of the artwork were immediately evident: (1) the boys and girls adhered closely to gender stereotypes (for example, the girls' themes conveyed a desire to "save the world," whereas boys drew weapons of mass destruction), and (2) the children manifested a need for a highly realistic, literal depiction of referents. Beyond these artistic qualities, the authors focus on the nature of children's communication with each other during their drawing sessions. This ongoing peer commentary, as well as self-narrative remarks, revealed examples of peer collaborative processes (see, for example, Teasley, 1995) that may influence children's artwork. Clearly, peer collaborative processes in children's artwork—a topic neglected by peer collaboration scholars—is a developmental phenomenon that warrants further scrutiny.

In Chapter Three, Watson and Schwartz investigate two important issues: (1) When does an artistic style emerge in children? and (2) What criteria do judges use to discern such artistic style? These scholars take the position that a style is evident when one person's art is consistent across different artworks and when that artist's work is distinct from another's artwork. Identifying the nature of style—its defining components and qualities—is a goal of the authors, who find that one-third of children have a discernible style. In comparisons between age groups, the authors find that distinctive styles may wax and wane as children age and develop in other domains.

In Chapter Four, Laible, Watson, and Koff present longitudinal evidence on a fascinating question: Do girls' drawings of people change as a result of menarche (a girl's first period)? This study spanned four years, allowing the authors to assess in six-month intervals changes in specific components of art across that time. Their findings suggest that artistic style may be more discernible across broader time intervals, but across the six months in which girls had their first period, artistic style was not discernible. This suggests that there may be sensitive periods in the development of style, that is, periods when development is sensitive to important psychological changes in the child.

In Chapter Five, Pufall and Pesonen discuss children's "artworlds" to address the *how* and the *what* of drawing. The authors do not define *style* in terms of a formal property of art or the thematic content of children's drawings. Rather, they claim that style is psychologically meaningful only when we consider "both how and what we draw." Their methodology for studying children's artistic style is intriguing. They use a *prospective* method to determine whether judges can perceive a style that persists in children's art as they get older; they also employ a *retrospective* approach to explore whether styles in older children's art allow judges to identify the same children's art when they were younger.

The chapters share many themes, yet within these overlaps are stimulating differences. For example, several chapters emphasize the social embeddedness of art. A broad cultural milieu offers fodder for children's drawing; as Pufall and Tesonen assert in their chapter, "artworlds" are always situated within cultural contexts. But there are also local influences—the important microsystems of the child's family and peer group. Several chapters in this volume investigate artistic development within these contexts.

The chapters offer a rich diversity in methodology. For example, several use longitudinal designs, which are potent for identifying phases of actual—rather than inferred—developmental sequences. Boyatzis presents a longitudinal case study of one girl from age two and one-half to six years;

Laible, Watson, and Koff study young adolescent girls over a four-year period; and Pufall and Tesonen analyze drawings by three children from the ages of five to nine years. Some of the work is highly naturalistic, that is, the researchers studied children in their home or school; other researchers collected drawings in more controlled circumstances.

The chapters also reflect diversity within the common ground of measuring artistic style. Several researchers rely on the *consensual assessment* technique in which multiple judges evaluate the same child's art. The researchers can then evaluate inter-judge agreement on individual children's style.

The chapters employ consensual assessment designs in innovative ways. For example, some analyze different drawings by one child during one time period; others use a prospective design in which judges use the stylistic features of early art to identify the children's later art; another method is a retrospective design in which judges use the stylistic features of later art and identify earlier drawings by the same child. Watson and Schwartz had judges rate features such as theme, saturation, and placement, as well as aesthetic appeal and creativity. Laible, Watson, and Koff asked judges to rate children's artistic ability and technical features such as detail and shading. Pufall and Tesonen had judges analyze thematic categories of animacy and events in children's art. In short, this volume offers much to researchers interested in style in art. Of course, the methods used here to assess artistic style could be applied to style in other domains.

Our hope is that this volume will motivate inquiry into social and symbolic facilitators and constraints in artistic development. Such work will enrich our understanding of the developmental sequences and processes, as well as the theoretical complexities in art. But the volume may have a value beyond enriching our knowledge of artistic development because the issues here—for example, the interplay of endogenous skill and social support, the nature of style, and continuity and discontinuity in development—are germane to many developmental domains.

Chris J. Boyatzis
Malcolm W. Watson
Editors

References

Fischer, K. W., and Bidell, T. R. "Dynamic Development of Psychological Structures in Action and Thought." In R. E. Lerner (ed.), *Theoretical Models of Human Development, Vol. 1: Handbook of Child Psychology* (W. Damon, series ed.). New York: Wiley, 1998.

Teasley, S. D. "The Role of Talk in Children's Peer Collaborations." *Developmental Psychology*, 1995, *31*, 207–220.

Vygotsky, L. S. *Mind in Society*. Cambridge, Mass.: Harvard University Press, 1978.

Wolf, D. P. "Development as the Growth of Repertoires." In M. B. Franklin and B. Kaplan (eds.), *Development and the Arts: Critical Perspectives*. Mahwah, N.J.: Erlbaum, 1994.

CHRIS J. BOYATZIS *is associate professor of psychology at Bucknell University in Lewisburg, Pennsylvania.*

MALCOLM W. WATSON *is professor of psychology at Brandeis University in Waltham, Massachusetts.*

1

A longitudinal case study illustrates how artistic development can be understood as the interplay between the child's developing symbolic skills and the contextual social support for the child's artistic expression.

The Artistic Evolution of Mommy: A Longitudinal Case Study of Symbolic and Social Processes

Chris J. Boyatzis

Children's art undergoes dramatic change during early childhood. Initially, children progress from making scribbles that lack representational intent to making graphic forms—circles, ovals, lines—that they do not use symbolically. Later the children give these forms symbolic meaning, often after the fact, when they recognize the forms' similarity to a referent. For example, a child may draw an oval and then declare, "balloon!"

Representational art emerges later, when children intentionally create graphic forms to represent a referent. In many children, drawing a human figure is the first clear symbol-referent artistic achievement. This early artistic development has often been assessed through a nomothetic approach with cross-sectional designs (Cox, 1993; Freeman, 1980; Golomb, 1974; Goodnow, 1977; Kellogg, 1970).

The case study, however, usually with a longitudinal design, also has a rich tradition and has been very useful for describing the stages, sequences, and microgenetic processes of art development (Cox and Parkin, 1986; Eng, 1931; Fein, 1976; Feinburg, 1976; Fenson, 1985; Gardner, 1980; Goldsmith, 1992; Golomb, 1992; Selfe, 1977; Smith, 1979; Zimmerman, 1992). Case studies effectively illustrate normative or atypical artistic development and identify the myriad forms symbolic expression can take. They also illuminate the seemingly paradoxical yet complementary qualities of flexibility and rigidity that are inherent in artistic and symbolic development; the cases generate hypotheses for subsequent research as well.

Overview of the Chapter

This chapter serves as an introduction for this volume by addressing general normative, theoretical, and methodological issues in artistic development, as well as broaching the more specific issues of symbolic and social constraints on artistic style.

I present a longitudinal case study of a girl, Janine, beginning when she was two and one-half years old. My emphasis is on the sequences of symbolic development in her art. Janine's drawings are constrained by her symbolic level, that is, her ability to create graphic equivalences between symbol and referent (in this case, her mother). Other factors influence her drawings as well, including her fine-motor and eye-hand coordination and mastery of the medium, which simultaneously constrain some qualities of artistic creation but give rise to others (Arnheim, 1954; Golomb, 1974). Such control of the medium is central to the emergence of artistic style (see Chapter Five of this volume). Competence in these components shapes the "process of bringing meanings to realization" (Smith, 1979, p. 60) in each drawing.

In addition to focusing on symbolic development, I address interpersonal and social constraints on artistic development. (Subsequent chapters will assess more systematically the impact of social constraints on children's art.) Adults often explicitly reward children's art ("What a nice picture!"), display the drawings at home and work, and suggest topics for new pictures. Adults may also model more advanced ways of depicting referents. Art educators (Chapman, 1978) have emphasized child-adult dialogue about the child's artwork as important communication and even as a catalyst to more advanced artistic forms. Recognizing these potential influences, some art scholars have argued that the study of a child's artistic development may actually be the study of artistic *socialization* with an adult "art collaborator" (Korzenik, 1992). This characterization may apply to many researchers who have been intimately involved with the artistic development of their subjects, sometimes their own children (see, for example, Feinburg, 1976; Fenson, 1985; Gardner, 1980; Goldsmith, 1992; Golomb, 1992; Zimmerman, 1992). Even Norman Freeman, long a student of endogenous and maturational influences on children's artistic development, has recently argued for thinking about children's human figure drawings in an interpersonal and contextual frame, claiming that the child understands and accepts a "social contract between artist and spectator" (Freeman, 1997, p. 32) that leads the child to create the kinds of drawings that trigger the viewer's recognition of the referent.

Korzenik (1992) suggests that dialogue between adult and child may compromise objectivity in studying children's art and even influence the art itself. However, such a close study would surely engender insights about the artistic process and product that may be precluded by a more detached, objective methodology. But adult-child interaction is also central theoretically to our understanding of artistic development. As Gauvain (1997) has argued, even if a child's behavior appears to be spontaneous, adults (developmentalists included) are likely to have a role in it, especially when they assume the complex position of observer-researcher-parent. Therefore, adults may indeed function as art collaborators and co-constructors of artistic development.

I elaborate next on these issues and relevant theoretical frameworks, such as Vygotsky's *zone of proximal development* (1978) and the notion of a *developmental range of skill* that is dependent on contextual support (Fischer and Bidell, 1998). I apply these theoretical constructs when particular drawings highlight their validity, and I also employ the orthogenetic principle as it applies to symbolic development (Werner and Kaplan, 1963).

Method

Like other studies of a single child's artistic development, this one has advantages typical of the case study (Mendelson, 1992). As an insider who is close to this child—once my subject, now my stepdaughter—I could make observations of her art development that were part of natural family interaction and discuss her art with her as she produced it. Hence I was an observer of not only the artistic product—the pictures—but also of the process, which was in many ways more interesting. Explicitly addressing these issues in this chapter is important because of the growing interest in the interplay of these aspects of art—the "what" and the "how" (see, for example, the fascinating study by Vinter, 1999). Surely, assessment of how children draw and their comments while drawing will provide insights that cannot be gleaned through scrutiny of the final product alone. (On verbalization in the drawing process, see Cocking and Copple, 1979; Gardner, Wolf, and Smith, 1982.) Also, due to the longitudinal nature of the study, I could observe artistic development unfold over time, including some fascinating instances of microgenesis, without needing to infer stages or sequences of development.

Subject, Setting, and Procedure. The subject of this study is a girl, Janine, who was two and one-half years old when the study began and who became my stepdaughter when she was five years old. Observations of Janine's drawing took place in her home, where she had access to many drawing materials. Most of her artwork was done spontaneously, although some drawing sessions were initiated by her mother or me. Drawing sessions usually lasted from five to ten minutes but were sometimes as brief as one minute or as long as thirty minutes. Throughout this study I was often directly involved with Janine's artistic behavior. Either after or during her drawing we sometimes discussed her art; I used a probing approach that avoids imposing meaning on the art and instead attempts to elicit the child's thoughts, interpretations, and feelings about it (Schirrmacher, 1986).

During the span of this study, Janine produced hundreds of pictures, with her mother as her most common subject. Thus Janine's thematic priority constituted a central element of her style and her artworld, as Pufall and Pesonen (this volume) might call it. Hence, I focus on the evolution of Janine's artistic representation of her mother. The particular drawings here were chosen because they are most representative of the child's artistic development throughout the corpus of her drawings and because they illustrate important developmental and theoretical issues.

Early Drawings. Beginning at about 2:6 (two years, six months), Janine drew many age-appropriate scribbles, identifying them as her mother, that showed no symbolic equivalence between the marks and their referent. At 2:7, Janine drew Figure 1.1 and said, "This is Mommy." Although the product suggests a faint likeness to a face, by viewing Janine's drawing process I could judge that she had no representational intent. Janine drew the oval and quickly added internal features in what seemed to be a random, unplanned fashion. Only after looking at the drawing for several seconds did she label it as her mother. This draw-and-label strategy is common for preschoolers who detect a picture's resemblance to a referent after drawing it (Gardner, 1980; Smith, 1979; Winner, 1982). For the next half year, Janine often used draw-and-label behavior.

In Figure 1.2 (drawn at age 3:4), Janine reaches an artistic milestone—an intentional, planned equivalence between symbol and referent. She employs and organizes the simplest of graphic conventions—the circle and line—that were prominent earlier but are now used to represent a person. This configuration—a circular form with internal details for facial features and vertical lines extending from the circle—is characteristic of preschoolers' first human figure drawings, commonly referred to as a tadpole person (Kellogg, 1970). Another common feature of this and Janine's other early humans is their frontal view, also typical in preschoolers' art.

Figure 1.1. Mommy by Janine at Age Two Years, Seven Months Intentional Representation

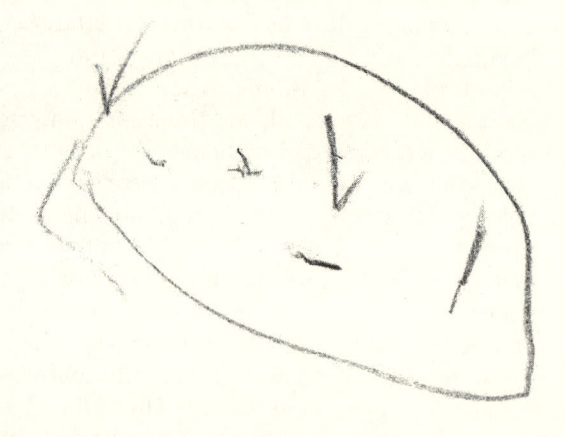

THE ARTISTIC EVOLUTION OF MOMMY   9

Figure 1.2. Mommy by Janine at Age Three Years, Four Months

Figure 1.2 shows that Janine not only comprehends but can produce representational marks on a page. When asked about her drawing, she described it as having a head with eyes, nose, and mouth; the jagged marks surrounding the head she labeled as mommy's hair.

The large circle that represents her mother's head illustrates the problem of relative size (Freeman, 1980). Common in preschoolers' drawings, the head is disproportionately large, perhaps due to its psychological salience (Di Leo, 1973) or the child's drawing strategies, such as Janine's tendency (shared by virtually all children) to draw the head first; consequently, all space is available for the head. When drawing the head first, children may also draw it so large because no other body parts are available to provide proportion. Although Vinter (1999) reports that preschoolers cannot plan globally and instead draw locally, segment to segment, others have found that when asked to draw a head on a torso already drawn, children draw a head with better proportions than when they first draw the head without a torso (Selfe, 1983; Thomas and Tsalimi, 1988). Another possibility credits the child with a planning strategy: Janine may draw the head disproportionately large because she anticipates placing facial features inside it (Freeman, 1980; Thomas and Tsalimi, 1988). Together, these issues highlight cognitive and symbolic constraints at work in children's drawing.

Despite the symbolic advances evident in Figure 1.2, the drawing omits many details—hands, feet, ears, the neck, and others. Such omissions are common in preschoolers' human figures. The torso is drawn distinctly in only 5 percent of four-year-olds' drawings; as many as half of preschoolers' drawings omit arms (Brown, 1990; Cox, 1993; Golomb, 1974). The reason for these omissions is uncertain. For example, the main circle in Figure 1.2 may represent the mother's head or, as Arnheim (1974) suggests, is a global, fused symbol for the head and torso combined. It is also possible that the vertical lines represent legs and the torso together. With regard to Figure 1.2, Janine said the horizontal lines crossing the leg lines were "Mommy's sweater," suggesting that she envisioned her mother's torso between the line legs. (Her mother was, in fact, wearing a striped sweater that day.) When asked to identify the torso on their tadpole persons, roughly half of preschoolers locate it within the space between the vertical lines; the remaining children place it within the head circle (Cox, 1993).

One of Cox's studies reveals a *body proportion effect*: children who draw a tadpole with a large head relative to the leg lines tend to claim the torso is within the head circle, whereas children who draw a tadpole with long legs relative to the head place the torso between the leg lines. It remains difficult to determine, however, whether children's placement of the torso is a hindsight interpretation in which they make sense of the picture's body parts after drawing them or whether they intend certain representations (such as drawing a long head contour to accommodate a torso).

Janine may have omitted the arms and torso due to a serial order effect in children's drawing: she attends to important structures at the drawing's beginning (the head) and end (the legs), and neglects structures in the middle (arms and torso) (Freeman, 1980). The absence of arms may also be due to cephalocaudal drawing sequences in which children begin with the head and then draw down the body (Bassett, 1977; Freeman, 1977). However, when asked to choose the best drawing of a person, tadpole-drawers prefer tadpole persons over more accurate, complete drawings of persons (Cox and Stone, cited in Cox, 1992). Thus preschoolers' affinity for tadpole persons may not be a memory or drawing artifact. The omission of arms may reflect the young child's internal model that consists, at this stage, only of the body's essential features in a strongly vertical axis: an elliptical circle as a head (and for some children, the torso) and, at the bottom, supportive lines as legs (and for some, the torso).

Over the next several months, Janine used the same tadpole form to represent different people: Janine's mother, father, grandmothers, and peers. This versatile tadpole (Figure 1.2) reflects an all-purpose schematic prototype that Janine used to represent people in general rather than in particular (Gardner, 1980). This artistic approach to rendering different people in strikingly similar ways suggests that Janine produces images that are evoked from an internal model consisting of the most salient and invariant features of the human figure. With symbolic maturity, the child's artistic depiction of the person becomes increasingly differentiated and complex, following a basic developmental trend outlined by early theorists (Piaget and Inhelder, 1956; Werner and Kaplan, 1963). Her artistic depictions also vary due to contextual demands, as we will see shortly.

Adding to her basic tadpole, Janine drew Figure 1.3 (at 3:5).

Increasing Differentiation in the Drawings. Arms are now included—a detail that emerged only after the depiction of the head, eyes, and legs (Figure 1.2); this sequence is common in preschoolers' human figure drawings (Cox, 1993; Gridley, 1938). But the arms in Figure 1.3 are perpendicular to the body, drawn in relation to their immediate ground—the straight lines used to depict mommy's legs.

Preschoolers often draw arms in perpendicular fashion, perhaps due to a poor understanding of verticality (Liben, 1981), often evident in children's drawing of chimneys perpendicular to the roof. This depiction is peculiar because preschoolers understand and perceive the horizontal rendition; they even prefer objects presented in their correct upright position rather than the perpendicular (Perner, Kohlmann, and Wimmer, 1984). A parsimonious explanation may be that the perpendicular arms result from Janine's use of the drawing strategy "to each its own space" (Goodnow, 1977, p. 40), in which the child avoids any overlapping of the boundaries of separate body parts.

Figure 1.3. Mommy by Janine at Age Three Years, Five Months

Figure 1.3 shows other changes from earlier pictures. For example, proportions are more accurate (leg lines are longer in relation to the head circle), and Janine has begun to write "Mommy" on her drawings, a practice she will continue for the next year. This behavior may reflect both Janine's desire to identify the drawing as her mother and her nascent writing ability, as many of Janine's first written words were labels on drawings. And Janine's mother seems to be floating; using labels and drawing floating people is common in early human figure drawings (Winner, 1982). Also her mother's hair is longer and fuller, indicating either that Janine is using the hair contour to represent the torso or that Janine is increasingly accurate in depicting her mother's very long hair.

Figure 1.4, drawn when Janine was 3:6, reflects a more fluid and better proportioned mother with a gradual inclusion of new body parts. The body parts are drawn more distinctly in their own space, though Janine said she erred by drawing three eyes (above the nose and mouth). Looking at Figure 1.4 with Janine, I asked about body parts she did not depict—specifically, eyelashes and brows, ears, teeth, belly button, and knees. This was a simple attempt to assess her knowledge of body parts and ability to draw them and to determine whether she could modify her human figure. Janine then drew Figure 1.5, which includes the parts I mentioned.

An interesting addition occurred when I mentioned her mother's belly button. Janine drew the large oval near the bottom of the hair contour for this part, but upon studying for a moment its disproportionately large size, Janine then added the smaller marks inside the oval. I asked about these markings, and she said the outer oval was her mother's tummy and the inner marks were her belly button. During this process, Janine reorganized her representation in an economical manner. She modified her existing schema and subsumed the stomach within a larger circle that was already available rather than alter her symbol in a more drastic way, such as by adding a torso section (see Karmiloff-Smith, 1990).

Janine's behavior also exemplifies a proportion effect when drawing the torso (Cox and Jarvis, cited in Cox, 1993), as Janine located the torso at the bottom of the proportionally large contour instead of between the smaller legs. Janine's torso placement in this enclosure indicates a change from two months earlier (Figure 1.2) when she located it between the leg lines.

Janine's inclusion and reasonable placement of many features in Figure 1.5 that were omitted in Figure 1.4 reflects her knowledge of and ability to draw body parts. This refutes the Piagetian notion that she would omit detailed body parts from spontaneous pictures (such as Figures 1.2, 1.3, and 1.4) because she has conceptual deficits or ignorance of body parts (Piaget and Inhelder, 1969). As young as two years, children possess knowledge of body parts, and three- to five-year-olds can draw them when asked, even if they do not include them in their spontaneous drawings (Golomb, 1974; Boyatzis, Michaelson, and Lyle, 1995). Nor does Janine omit body parts because she suffers from production difficulties (Freeman, 1980; Goodnow,

THE ARTISTIC EVOLUTION OF MOMMY   13

Figure 1.4. Mommy by Janine at Age Three Years, Six Months

Figure 1.5. Mommy Revised by Janine at Age Three Years, Six Months

1977). As Figure 1.5 shows, Janine can draw body parts and draw them in their correct location. She may have omitted them previously because she, like many young children, draws top-to-bottom, starting at the top of the person and including the most important features (head, eyes) and ending with the legs. By the time the child comes to the bottom of the drawing, she has a sense that she has finished the person (see Goodnow, 1977, and Van Sommers, 1984, on graphic production rules). Unfortunately, the precise order in which Janine drew body parts was not recorded. However, I suspect that more important than a drawing sequence is Janine's internal model of a human figure and what she considers its essential features. Preschoolers judge the "global likeness sufficient" (Golomb, 1974, p. 60) as a person, and their human figure drawings may be to them (despite their appearance to adults as deficient) adequate graphic symbols that do not require a "point-by-point isomorphism between the drawing and its referent" (Gardner, 1980, p. 63). The simple renditions in Figures 1.2, 1.3, and 1.4 express unequivocally to Janine, "This is Mommy." Such drawings may serve as a cognitive or symbolic shorthand (Golomb, 1981) that concisely conveys the referent, with a balance and symmetry that is aesthetically pleasing (Kellogg, 1970).

Like prior pictures, Figures 1.4 and 1.5 indicate that Janine respects the drawing rule that different body parts should not violate each other's space (Goodnow, 1977). The limb lines usually stop at the boundaries of other parts. Janine's drawings suggest that violations of this drawing rule may occur more when certain body parts require fine-motor control at the edge of the child's skill. Perhaps the arms' horizontal lines, made by the child's lower arm and hand moving laterally (or just a wrist movement), are easier to draw than vertical leg lines, which require the child's entire arm to retract the drawing hand toward the body. Figure 1.4 suggests this. Interestingly, the no-overlapping rule (and other drawing strategies) may be more vulnerable when the child is intent on creating new forms. This occurred in Figure 1.5, when Janine drew many new body parts but had the arms violate the hair line. In contrast, Figure 1.4 did not include the challenge of creating new forms, and in that picture Janine respected the hair line boundary. One lesson from this case study is that it is not easy to find hard-and-fast drawing rules; what appear to be distinct drawing strategies may be more random than ordered, or at least indicative of a cognitive flexibility in this domain.

Drawing in the Zone of Proximal Development. The contrast between Janine's spontaneous (Figures 1.2, 1.3, and 1.4) and elicited artwork (Figure 1.5) illuminates important developmental and theoretical issues. Figure 1.5 reveals that Janine's optimal symbolic performance exceeds that displayed in her spontaneous drawing (Figure 1.4) that she had created just moments earlier. The discrepancy between the higher and lower artistic levels was due to the support and elicitation in my requests and encouragement. Janine's performance in a given picture seems to be a function of the degree of support or scaffolding from the environment. If so, perhaps artistic skill level ought to be conceived not in terms of either the modal (functional) drawing level or the highest (optimal) level. Rather, artistic skill may be better conceptualized as that *range of symbolic flexibility* between the two levels (see Fischer and Bidell, 1998; Kitchener and Fischer, 1990).

This view is integral to Vygotsky's notion of the *zone of proximal development*, that is, the distance between a child's "actual developmental level as determined by independent problem solving" and the "potential development as determined through problem solving under adult guidance or in collaboration with more capable peers" (1978, p. 86). This region of sensitivity or range of symbolic flexibility may have a baseline of functional skill in spontaneous and unsupported contexts and a ceiling of optimal skill expressed in scaffolded or elicited conditions. In artistic development, this zone or range shifts gradually upward with the child's physical and symbolic maturation and increasing mastery of media; nevertheless, the optimal skill manifested at any age is influenced by context. In a related vein, Wolf (1994, 1997; Wolf and Perry, 1988) has made the cogent argument that a child's artistic development be conceptualized not as the highest skill displayed with reference to some artistic *telos* but as the repertoire of skills available to produce different renditions called for in different contexts. This issue is revisited at the end of the chapter.

The striking differences between Janine's drawings in a spontaneous versus scaffolded context led to a study (Boyatzis, Michaelson, and Lyle, 1995) to test whether preschoolers could be trained to include more body parts in their drawings. Preschoolers were asked to draw a person and then were assigned to a support condition. Children were asked to either point to body parts on themselves as the experimenter read a list of them aloud or to draw the parts on a snowman-shaped outline. After completing this task, children drew another person, which was compared to the first drawing to determine how the support conditions influenced the children's human figures. Overall, children's second drawings were similar to their first, suggesting that their human figures were relatively immune to our attempts to improve them.

A subsequent study (Boyatzis, Lavan, and Jacobs, 1997) assessed the effects of other support conditions. The results show that children who receive some form of support modify their drawings more than control children do but that they do not change them much in any absolute sense; the most modification occurs when children discuss their first drawing with an adult (for example, "Say you want to add ears to your person; where would they go?"). Together these findings support the idea that young children's artistic flexibility depends on the specific support children receive. Many studies converge on this conclusion (for example, Barrett and Bridson, 1983; Cox, 1978; Lewis, Russell, and Berridge, 1993; Light and McEwen, 1987; Zhi, Thomas, and Robinson, 1997).

It seems, then, that artistic skill could be recast in terms of the interplay between emergent abilities and context-dependent factors (see Fischer and Bidell, 1998; Karmiloff-Smith, 1990). However, it is likely that some children modify their drawings because their functional, spontaneous level is beginning to mature to greater differentiation in human figures. Thus artistic development in general and specifically the expression of stylistic qualities may have sensitive periods. These issues are explored in the chapter by Laible, Watson, and Koff (this volume) on girls' drawings before and after menarche.

Personal Meaning and Problem Solving in the Drawings. Although there is variability in how Janine draws her mother, it is clear that Janine's increasing mastery in symbolically depicting her mother allows her to commence a period of personally meaningful creativity and experimentation in her art. Her drawings from ages 4:1 to 4:4 reflect various symbolic changes. Janine drew her mother engaged in activities and in activities she shared with Janine. Figure 1.6, drawn when Janine was 4:1, is Janine's first drawing that depicts her and her mother together; it also is the first depiction of action by Janine's mother.

Janine drew the several curved lines on the paper above and to the right of her own head with emphatic swings of her hand, striking the paper with the marker. While doing so, she uttered, "Mommy's *patting* my head, she's *patting* my head," illustrating the role of gestural enhancement to convey the picture's meaning. (Werner and Kaplan, 1963, and Wolf, 1994, offer fas-

Figure 1.6. Mommy by Janine at Age Four Years, One Month

cinating analyses of the significance of gesture in early art.) The product itself fails to capture the personal significance of this drawing, which is underscored by the gestural component. As Wolf (1994) notes, gestural components may be meaningful to the artist but "can be imperceptible to perceivers who encounter only the final swath of the marks" (p. 70). Appreciating the emotional significance of this drawing and observing the child's attempt to integrate meaning with making is achieved only due to the close observation of the drawing process.

In Figure 1.6, Janine symbolically depicts herself and her mother with virtually identical graphic components; the only distinction between the two is expressed through a size differential. This thriftiness in symbolic components (Goodnow, 1977) is common and reflects young children's use of generic prototypes that capture people's essential elements. As Janine focuses on animating her mother and capturing an important event, the mother has lost a few qualities (her hands and feet) from drawings done even half a year earlier (Figures 1.4 and 1.5), and the no-overlap rule is violated. The picture is busier than earlier ones, and the goal of graphically representing the interpersonal action ("*patting* my head") may have diverted energy from other details she had mastered earlier. If so, the child has demonstrated a variability in the goals of her drawing, with attention shifting from one (drawing to capture a graphic equivalence between symbol and referent) to another (drawing to capture personal meaning). Also the progression from representation of "other" (Figures 1.2 through 1.5) to representation of "other with self" (Figure 1.6) reflects an increasing differentiation and integration in her artwork.

Although reproduced in black and white, Figure 1.7, drawn at 4:2, is Janine's first drawing with different colors to distinguish herself from her mother. Also her mother's arms are not only hanging down but one is placed around Janine. As Janine drew she said, "Mommy is mushing [hugging] me."

This drawing, like Figure 1.6 drawn at 4:1, conveys interpersonal and emotional meaning for the child artist. Although drawn one month after Figure 1.6, Figure 1.7 includes squiggly coil-like lines for hands and feet on Janine and her mother. Perhaps as Janine has become more comfortable with depicting action, some details (hands, feet) that were absent a month earlier return. This progression suggests, as did earlier ones, that the child has a variability of goals and strategies at work in her art.

At age 4:3 Janine drew Figure 1.8, which she described as "Mommy and Janine holding balloons, and I'm holding a candy cane upside down."

As in many other pictures at this age, Janine is interested in endowing drawings with personal meaning and positive affect, as she depicts important activities shared with her mother. As is typical for her age, Janine distorted an object to make it fit the space available by drawing some balloons horizontally. This tactic supports the description of the young artist as a problem solver who generates solutions, albeit erroneous at times, to graphic problems (Goodnow, 1977).

Figure 1.7. Mommy by Janine at Age Four Years, Two Months

Figure 1.8. Mommy by Janine at Age Four Years, Three Months

An Instance of Microgenesis. It is exciting to observe microgenetic change while watching children draw. Figures 1.9 and 1.10 were drawn within moments of each other when Janine was 4:2. Figure 1.9 presents a "stripped-down" mother, with much of the richness and fluidity of earlier drawings missing. However, for the first time, Janine drew her mother's arms hanging *down* (albeit too far) rather than perpendicular to her body. (Janine told me that the outer lines were arms and the inner lines were legs.) However, the picture reflects some symbolic regression, as her mother has lost her abundant hair and smile. The link between this arm correction and regression of the drawing's overall quality suggests that Janine is focusing on a specific graphic element. Around this age Janine's drawings of other people also possess the arm-to-the-floor feature, indicating that she is intent on exploring a single drawing unit (see Fenson, 1985).

Subsequent drawings might provide the answer to whether her focus on the arms caused the disruption in her mother's other features, even ones as well established as her mother's hair. If the arms assume a more appropriate length, would her mother's overall richness return?

Immediately after drawing Figure 1.9, Janine drew Figure 1.10. Her mother's arms now have a more accurate length, and her hair and vivid smile have returned. It seems that as Janine reconciled the arm-length challenge, other elements that had been disturbed in Figure 1.9 are now restored, which suggests that a symbolic equilibration had been reached in

Figure 1.9. Mommy by Janine at Age Four Years, Two Months

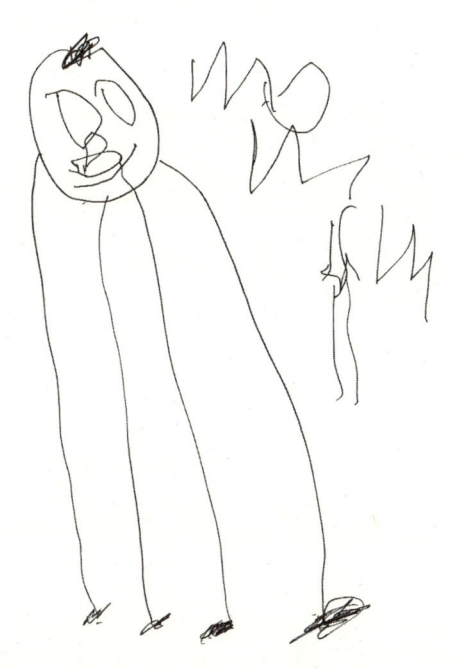

Figure 1.10. Mommy by Janine at Age Four Years, Two Months

this moment of microgenesis. And as in earlier drawings, these latest ones manifest Janine's adherence to drawing rules. In Figure 1.10 Janine heeds the rule "to each its own space," as she restores her mother's hairline by encircling the head but halts a fraction of an inch before touching the vertical lines representing her mother's arms.

Later drawings, from 4:9 to 5:1, reflect increasing differentiation and organization of the human figure. Figure 1.11, drawn when she was 4:9, includes several innovations. Janine uses for the first time an identifiable and distinct torso. The torso appears in most children's human figure drawings by five years (Cox, 1993); drawing it as a separate unit from the head is typical for this age (Fenson, 1985).

The torso's triangular shape is common, especially for depicting the female torso. Figure 1.11 reflects Janine's progression in depicting limbs initially with single lines to the later use of distinct enclosed segments. This evolution continues later. And though not visible here, Janine uses color to distinguish body parts. The hair is brown, facial features blue and red, and the spots on her mother's legs green—for the green shorts her mother wore that day.

This figure represents the first time Janine colors in a drawing. It also indicates an improved proportionality and control over the entire symbol of human figures. And the figure suggests that the anticipated presence of

Figure 1.11. Mommy by Janine at Age Four Years, Nine Months

other parts (such as a separate torso) leads to better proportions rather than that the head's emotional salience might have diminished or that it was drawn so large previously to accommodate facial features.

Over the several months after her fifth birthday, Janine embarked on a series of graphic experiments. Her many drawings around this time all display an intentional manipulation of her artistic symbol. For example, she drew her mother "in Mexico," "in Japan," "with hair blowing in her face," "being green," and "with the short hair." In the last example, her use of the article *the* suggests that she consciously varied that component of her symbol. Taken together, this period of drawing and the verbalizations that accompanied them indicate that perhaps after refining her graphic representation of her mother, Janine was comfortable experimenting with her artistic symbol in creating variations on the Mommy theme.

With greater symbolic competence came Janine's use of art to convey emotions. Figure 1.12, drawn at 5:3, depicts a woman with a broad smile and enlarged abdomen, and a small girl without a mouth (and therefore lacking the smile ubiquitous in Janine's drawings).

Shortly afterward Janine said, "The woman is having a baby, and the little girl is worried." Later that day Janine confessed in a somber tone that the

Figure 1.12. Mommy by Janine at Age Five Years, Three Months

woman represented her mother and the little girl represented herself. Although her mother was not pregnant nor was discussing becoming so, Janine's art indirectly communicated her feelings about the prospect of that happening. Also the legs are drawn not as single lines, as in her earlier pictures, but as enclosed segments. This progression to using enclosed space for limbs appears around age five (Cox, 1993).

Figures 1.13, 1.14, and 1.15 reflect increasing differentiation and organization of the human figure. Figure 1.13 (drawn when Janine was 5:10) depicts for the first time a distinct neck, enclosed and segmented legs, and the appearance of scenery that commonly emerges in five- to seven-year-olds' art.

Figure 1.14, drawn at 6:2, depicts Janine (bottom), her mother (left), and her stepfather (me, the author, whose head is distinctly in the wrong place). Changes include using rigidly segmented and geometric body parts. Janine also tries to draw the feet so as to create depth and perspective. This drawing shows how Janine is now experimenting with different representations of the human figure: her mother's torso and arms are drawn in one continuous segment, whereas my body has separate sections for the neck, arms, upper chest, abdomen, and hands. In this drawing Janine depicts for the first time hands as enclosed units rather than lines radiating from the limb. And her own body is drawn in a symbolic style that is more similar to her earlier drawings (for example, Figure 1.13) than to the other human figures in this same picture (Figure 1.14). The variability within this drawing's depiction of different bodies reflects what could be either a playful flexibility in constructing graphic symbols or a very intentional and controlled vari-

THE ARTISTIC EVOLUTION OF MOMMY   23

Figure 1.13. Mommy by Janine at Age Five Years, Ten Months

Figure 1.14. Mommy by Janine at Age Six Years, Two Months

ation on a theme. To choose among these different characterizations it would help to ask the child artist about such issues. Unfortunately I did not. In either case, it appears that the child, at any one time period and even within seconds of drawing different people, employs multiple drawing strategies and solutions to the challenge of graphically depicting the human figure.

Figure 1.15. Mommy by Janine at Age Six Years, Five Months

this is mom Holding Ballons

The final picture (Figure 1.15), drawn when Janine was 6:5, reflects a new integration of specific components. Some earlier features remain, such as her mother engaged in a significant (to Janine) activity, body parts drawn so as not to overlap, and the feet drawn for depth. But facial features are more detailed; the neck and torso make up one continuous segment; there is distinct clothing, with the arms coming out from under the clothing; the arms, hands, and legs are enclosed segments; and the hands are more refined than previously. Earlier qualities are retained and integrated anew in more complex and later-emerging organizations.

Conclusions

During this longitudinal case study, the child's symbolic depiction of her mother evolved from initial scribbles and draw-and-label forms at around two and one-half years of age, to representational tadpole persons, and later to a detailed human figure engaged in meaningful activity. Throughout these changes the drawings show a trend, consistent with the orthogenetic principle, toward increasing differentiation and integration in the symbolic construction. Overall, Janine's drawings of her mother became increasingly detailed, with earlier components and forms integrated into the newly emerging drawings. In another trend, Janine first depicted her mother alone and then with the child herself, and still later with other people. At the level of specific body parts, the symbolic expression changed dramatically, such as in representing limbs, with a progression from a single line to an enclosed segment to a continuous contour. These graphic changes manifest the child's ongoing symbolic changes toward increasing differentiation and integration. Lest these remarks imply that the evolution of Mommy reveals only an upward progression in symbolic expression, we see throughout these changes many signs of a cognitive variability and flexibility.

Many social constraints were apparent during this longitudinal case. The observer-researcher served as an art collaborator—a co-constructor who seemingly influenced the child's artistic development while studying it. But this special case of social constraint seems to have sometimes benefited the child artist, as it engendered more complex expression and organization at several points in the case study. This effect is clearly seen in the symbolic transition from Figure 1.4 to 1.5. This closeness between child artist and observer also facilitated the observer's analysis of not only product but process, including some fascinating microgenetic changes that are especially apparent in the progressions from Figure 1.4 to 1.5 and from Figure 1.9 to 1.10.

The close observation of the drawing process, and indeed a direct and verbal involvement with the process, generated insights about constraints on artistic development. For example, there is evidence here that early drawing development is constrained by different rules and strategies, but there appears to be a flexibility in the child's application of such rules. One consequence is that we might avoid characterizing children as rule users and problem solvers in any rigid sense and might instead attempt to explain the interplay of the flexible employment of rules within the child's repertoire of skills. Variation in children's adherence to rules could be judged as merely random: sometimes they follow rules, and sometimes they don't. Or we could see this variability as a more theoretically significant commingling of different strategies and styles—a symbolic variability that may be an essential feature of cognitive growth (see, for example, Siegler, 1995).

Throughout the analysis of Janine's drawings, I have spoken in terms of different stages or progressions of artistic development—scribbling to tadpole persons and so on, or a single line to enclosed segment to continuous contour for a limb. This presumption of stages carries a risk of oversimplification. If Janine and other children demonstrate a symbolic variability that is meaningful and perhaps even intentional, then we might consider how children possess "multiple ways of thinking [or drawing] at any one time" (Siegler, 1995, p. 266). At any one chronological point, artistic skill may be more variable than constrained by some coherent, stage-like organization. Over time, earlier drawing components are not always replaced by later-emerging, more mature ones but are often integrated into forms that evolve in their meaning, "growing up . . . in one another's presence" (Wolf, 1994, p. 75). These interpretations of Janine's artistic development are surely consistent with the orthogenetic principle of increasing differentiation and organization—a principle that some (Kaplan, 1994) suggest is crucial for understanding development in art. Data from other studies (for example, Cox and Parkin, 1986) also suggest that art-stage presumptions are problematic, as stage-like transitions vary dramatically within and between children. Variability seems the rule rather than the exception. Thus, rather than interpret the child's level at any one time as stage-like and coherent, it may be best to conceptualize level and skill in terms of a *range* of skills or a "spectrum of possibilities," as Wolf (1997, p. 192) puts it. The expression of any one artistic skill, in thematic preference or technical style, will be influenced by the specific social context in which the child is drawing. Vygotsky (1978) describes this range in terms of actual versus potential skill—a zone of proximal development that is bordered by the degree of support from more capable others. Fischer and Bidell (1998) elaborate on this conceptualization, noting that "real behaviors . . . function not at a single level but in a range or zone" (p. 486), and the expression of skill within that zone is shaped by contextual factors (social support, task demands, and so on).

An eloquent call for a "reimagining" of development comes from Dennie Wolf (1994; 1997; Wolf and Perry, 1988), who posits the hypothetical constructs of *choice* and *diversity* within the child's *repertoire* rather than notions of linear progression and coherence and replacement of earlier forms by later, more mature forms (the latter presumptions being central to traditional stage theories of development). Wolf (1994) likes the term *repertoire* and reminds us of Darwin's image of the "branching coral." Fischer and Bidell (1998) speak of a "constructive web" to capture the salience of variability in developmental skill. The use of the term *evolution* in the title of this chapter is a nod to the parallel dialectic that exists between older and newer notions of development and between the stage-like progress and variability that Janine evinces. If we adapt these models and metaphors of development, we are called to understand the interplay between the child's skills and the aspects and effects of the psychologically meaningful environment. My sense is that a fruitful model of artistic development entails an artistic freedom and potential that operates within symbolic and social limits. Some models (such as Wolf's) emphasize the child's inherent diversity of skill and surrounding contextual facilitators of the skill. If we accept a repertoire model, then we see the child as possessing, at any one time, diverse artistic competencies and as choosing from their repertoire, like drawing one arrow from a quiver, depending on what the particular context, audience, or task calls for. But we need to understand better this interplay of artistic freedom and context.

It could be that, due to the child's endogenous limits and contextual constraints, the child's repertoire and developmental range and zone all have a ceiling (recall here Mark Twain's crack that "you can't teach a pig to sing"). If skill is, as Fischer and Bidell (1998) claim, *in media res*—in the middle between child and context—the child's range or zone of skill is theoretically upwardly boundless because of the environment's potential of devising new and improved guidance and inspiration of higher skills in the child. Let us look forward to deeper understanding of how child and context interact to influence development in art and other developmental domains.

References

Arnheim, R. *Art and Visual Perception.* Berkeley: University of California, 1954.
Barrett, M. D., and Bridson, A. "The Effect of Instructions on Children's Drawings." *British Journal of Developmental Psychology,* 1983, *1,* 175–178.
Bassett, E. "Production Strategies in the Child's Drawing of the Human Figure." In G. Butterworth (ed.), *The Child's Representation of the World.* New York: Plenum, 1977.
Boyatzis, C. J., Lavan, S. K., and Jacobs, C. "Symbolic Flexibility in Children's Drawings of the Human Figure." Poster presented at the biennial meeting of the Society for Research in Child Development, Washington, D.C., Apr. 1997.
Boyatzis, C. J., Michaelson, P., and Lyle, E. "Symbolic Immunity and Flexibility in Preschoolers' Human Figure Drawings." *Journal of Genetic Psychology,* 1995, *156,* 293–302.
Brown, E. V. "Developmental Characteristics of Figure Drawings Made by Boys and Girls Ages Five Through Eleven." *Perceptual and Motor Skills,* 1990, *70,* 279–288.
Chapman, L. C. *Approaches to Art Education.* Orlando, Fla.: Harcourt Brace, 1978.
Cocking, R. R., and Copple, C. E. "Change Through Exposure to Others: A Study of Children's Verbalizations as They Draw." In M. K. Poulsen and G. I. Lubin (eds.), *Piagetian Theory and Its Implications for the Helping Professions.* University Park: University of Southern California Press, 1979.
Cox, M. V. "Spatial Depth Relationships in Young Children's Drawings." *Journal of Experimental Child Psychology,* 1978, *26,* 551–554.
Cox, M. V. *Children's Drawings.* Harmondsworth, England: Penguin, 1992.
Cox, M. V. *Children's Drawings of the Human Figure.* Mahwah, N.J.: Erlbaum, 1993.
Cox, M. V., and Parkin, C. "Young Children's Human Figure Drawing: Cross-Sectional and Longitudinal Studies." *Educational Psychology,* 1986, *6,* 353–368.
Di Leo, J. H. *Children's Drawings as Diagnostic Aids.* New York: Brunner/Mazel, 1973.
Eng, H. *The Psychology of Children's Drawings.* London: Routledge, 1931.
Fein, S. *Heidi's Horse.* Pleasant Hill, Calif.: Exelrod, 1976.
Feinburg, S. G. "Combat in Child Art." In J. S. Bruner, A. Jolly, and K. Sylva (eds.), *Play: Its Role in Development and Evolution.* New York: Basic Books, 1976.
Fenson, L. "The Transition from Construction to Sketching in Children's Drawing." In N. F. Freeman and M. Cox (eds.), *Visual Order: The Nature and Development of Pictorial Representations.* Cambridge, England: Cambridge University Press, 1985.
Fischer, K. W., and Bidell, T. R. "Dynamic Development of Psychological Structures in Action and Thought." In R. E. Lerner (ed.), *Theoretical Models of Human Development, Vol. 1: Handbook of Child Psychology* (W. Damon, series ed.). New York: Wiley, 1998.
Freeman, N. H. "How Young Children Try to Plan Drawings." In G. Butterworth (ed.), *The Child's Representation of the World.* New York: Plenum, 1977.
Freeman, N. H. *Strategies of Representation in Young Children.* Orlando, Fla.: Academic Press, 1980.
Freeman, N. H. "Identifying Resources from Which Children Advance into Pictorial Innovation." *Journal of Aesthetic Education,* 1997, *31,* 23–33.
Gardner, H. *Artful Scribbles.* New York: Basic Books, 1980.
Gardner, H., Wolf, D. P., and Smith, A. "Max and Molly: Individual Differences in Early Artistic Symbolization." In H. Gardner (ed.), *Art, Mind, and Brain.* New York: Basic Books, 1982.

Gauvain, M. "Lessons from Children: Observations by Developmental Psychologists at Home." *SRCD Newsletter,* 1997, *40,* 3–4, 8–9.
Goldsmith, L. T. "Wang Yani: Stylistic Development of a Chinese Painting Prodigy." *Creativity Research Journal,* 1992, *5,* 281–293.
Golomb, C. *Young Children's Sculpture and Drawing: A Study in Representational Development.* Cambridge, Mass.: Harvard University, 1974.
Golomb, C. "Representation and Reality: The Origins and Determinants of Young Children's Drawings." *Review of Research in Visual Art Education,* 1981, *14,* 36–48.
Golomb, C. "Eytan: The Early Development of a Gifted Child Artist." *Creativity Research Journal,* 1992, *5,* 265–279.
Goodnow, J. *Children Drawing.* Cambridge, Mass.: Harvard University Press, 1977.
Gridley, P. F. "Graphic Representation of a Man by Four-Year-Old Children in Nine Prescribed Drawing Situations." *Genetic Psychology Monographs,* 1938, *20,* 183–350.
Kaplan, B. "Is a Concept of Development Applicable to the Arts?" In M. B. Franklin and B. Kaplan (eds.), *Development and the Arts: Critical Perspectives.* Mahwah, N.J.: Erlbaum, 1994.
Karmiloff-Smith, A. "Constraints on Representational Change: Evidence from Children's Drawing." *Cognition,* 1990, *34,* 57–83.
Kellogg, R. *Analyzing Children's Art.* Mountain View, Calif.: Mayfield, 1970.
Kitchener, K. S., and Fischer, K. W. "A Skill Approach to the Development of Reflective Thinking." In D. Kuhn (ed.), *Developmental Perspectives on Teaching and Learning Thinking Skills.* New York: Karger, 1990.
Korzenik, D. "Gifted Child Artists." *Creativity Research Journal,* 1992, *5,* 313–319.
Lewis, C., Russell, C., and Berridge, D. "When Is a Mug Not a Mug? Effects of Content, Naming, and Instructions on Children's Drawing." *Journal of Experimental Child Psychology,* 1993, *56,* 291–302.
Liben, L. "Copying and Reproducing Pictures in Relation to Subjects' Operative Levels." *Developmental Psychology,* 1981, *17,* 357–365.
Light, P., and McEwen, F. "Drawings as Messages: The Effect of a Communication Game upon Production of View-Specific Drawings." *British Journal of Developmental Psychology,* 1987, *5,* 53–60.
Mendelson, M. J. "Let's Teach Case Methods to Developmental Students." *SRCD Newsletter,* Fall 1992, pp. 9, 13.
Perner, J., Kohlmann, R., and Wimmer, H. "Young Children's Recognition and Use of the Vertical and Horizontal in Drawings." *Child Development,* 1984, *55,* 1637–1645.
Piaget, J., and Inhelder, B. *The Child's Conception of Space.* London: Routledge, 1956.
Piaget, J., and Inhelder, B. *The Psychology of the Child.* New York: Basic Books, 1969.
Schirrmacher, R. "Talking with Young Children About Their Art." *Young Children,* July 1986, pp. 3–7.
Selfe, L. *Nadia.* Orlando, Fla.: Harcourt Brace, 1977.
Selfe, L. *Normal and Anomalous Representational Drawing Ability in Children.* London: Academic Press, 1983.
Siegler, R. S. "How Does Change Occur? A Microgenetic Study of Number Conservation." *Cognitive Psychology,* 1995, *28,* 225–273.
Smith, N. R. "How a Picture Means." In H. Gardner and D. P. Wolf (eds.), *Early Symbolization.* New Directions for Child Development, no. 3. San Francisco: Jossey-Bass, 1979.
Thomas, G. V., and Tsalimi, A. "Effects of Order Drawing Head and Trunk on Their Relative Sizes in Children's Human Figure Drawings." *British Journal of Developmental Psychology,* 1988, *6,* 191–203.
Van Sommers, P. *Drawing and Cognition.* Cambridge, England: Cambridge University Press, 1984.
Vinter, A. "How Meaning Modifies Drawing Behavior in Children." *Child Development,* 1999, *70,* 33–49.

Vygotsky, L. S. *Mind in Society: The Development of Higher Psychological Processes.* Cambridge, Mass.: Harvard University Press, 1978.

Werner, H., and Kaplan, B. *Symbol Formation.* New York: Wiley, 1963.

Winner, E. *Invented Worlds: The Psychology of the Arts.* Cambridge, Mass.: Harvard University Press, 1982.

Wolf, D. P. "Development as the Growth of Repertoires." In M. B. Franklin and B. Kaplan (eds.), *Development and the Arts: Critical Perspectives.* Mahwah, N.J.: Erlbaum, 1994.

Wolf, D. P. "Reimagining Development: Possibilities from the Study of Children's Art." *Human Development,* 1997, *40,* 189–194.

Wolf, D. P., and Perry, M. D. "From Endpoints to Repertoires: Some New Conclusions About Drawing Development." In H. Gardner and D. N. Perkins (eds.), *Art, Mind, and Education: Research from Project Zero.* Urbana: University of Illinois Press, 1988.

Zhi, Z., Thomas, G. V., and Robinson, E. J. "Constraints on Representational Change: Drawing a Man with Two Heads." *British Journal of Developmental Psychology,* 1997, *15,* 275–290.

Zimmerman, E. "Factors Influencing the Graphic Development of a Talented Young Artist." *Creativity Research Journal,* 1992, *5,* 295–311.

CHRIS J. BOYATZIS is associate professor of psychology at Bucknell University in Lewisburg, Pennsylvania. His primary research interests are children's artistic development and religious and spiritual development.

2

There are striking gender differences in boys' and girls' artistic styles. A naturalistic observation of children drawing sheds light on the sociocognitive and collaborative processes through which peers influence each other's art.

A Naturalistic Observation of Children Drawing: Peer Collaboration Processes and Influences in Children's Art

Chris J. Boyatzis, Gretchen Albertini

Some years ago, a *Calvin and Hobbes* cartoon by Bill Watterson captured a robust difference between boys' and girls' art. In that strip Calvin asked his antagonist, Susie, what she drew in art class; looking at her picture Calvin remarked, "Well, a tidy little domestic scene. A house in a yard with flowers. How typically female." In the next frame Calvin declared, "Girls think small and are preoccupied with petty details. But *boys* think *big*! Boys think about action and accomplishment! No wonder it's men who change the world!" When Susie asks Calvin what he drew, he proudly replies, "A squadron of B-1s nuking New York." The cartoon captures two themes of this chapter: (1) gender differences in children's art and (2) the nature of peer influence on that art.

During the elementary school years, boys and girls indeed produce very different artwork (Cox, 1993; Feinburg, 1977; Lange-Küttner and Edelstein, 1995; Machover, 1960; McNiff, 1982; Reeves and Boyette, 1983; Rubenstein and Rubin, 1984). Gender differences in art emerge even earlier, in the preschool years, as boys' scribbles are rated as more masculine and girls' scribbles as more feminine by judges who are ignorant of the children's genders (Boyatzis and Eades, 1999; Boyatzis and Parisella, 2000).

But the focus here is on the school years, when children create representational art with elaborate pictures. Boys often draw themes of power, competition, and depersonalized aggression, using monsters, vehicles, and weapons. Compared to girls' drawings, boys' characters are drawn further apart; they are also in profile and in motion. Girls typically draw static images of natural settings with people and animals; people are often drawn with facial and bodily detail and in an inactive, frontal view.

In one study of eight- to eleven-year-olds who drew pictures of water, girls drew calm rivers and oceans and boys drew storms at sea (Kawecki, 1994). As style consists of not only thematic content but of technical drawing qualities (Somerville, 1983), there are technical differences between boys' and girls' art. During the school years boys draw angular, geometric shapes, whereas girls are likely to produce curvier, organic forms. Girls' drawings feature more detail, decoration, and sexual markers (features that convey the sex of the human figure).

When girls are asked to draw people helping and fighting others (Feinburg, 1977), their drawings feature a personalized quality, focusing on individuals. When boys receive the same instruction, their drawings have a depersonalized quality, with more structured group events. For example, when second and third graders drew pictures of fighting, boys drew organized group conflicts such as sports contests or war; characters' identities were often concealed by helmets, equipment, or armor. In contrast, girls represented interpersonal conflicts, such as confrontations between friends or family members, without concealing faces or identities. Taken together, these findings demonstrate differences in the stylistic essences of *what* and *how* boys and girls draw.

In the sense of style that Somerville (1983) offers, we see that boys and girls are different from each other in subject matter, technical form, and meaning. In this chapter, however, such gender differences are used as a tool or lens to help us understand social processes between peers that may influence what school children draw.

Sources of Gender Differences in Art

Several theories account for gender differences in children's art. In early childhood, gender schemas develop and organize gender-related information (Basow, 1992). Gender schemas crystallize and exaggerate children's gender socialization, which could increase the expression of gender-appropriate content in drawings.

The present chapter addresses not cognitive but social factors, which have been stressed as a cause of artistic gender differences (Cox, 1993). There are differences in boys' and girls' socialization experiences due to societal norms (Block, 1984; Pomerleau, Bolduc, Malcuit, and Cossette, 1990; Thorne, 1986, 1993)—differences that are likely to influence children's art, as the earlier description of boys' and girls' drawings shows them to be in accord with societal gender stereotypes.

The influence of cultural milieu on art is highlighted by a finding from an East Indian Island, which claims that, in contrast to Western children's art, girls draw pictures of tools four times more than boys do, who draw humans, flowers, and spirits to a greater extent than girls do (Lark-Horovitz,

Lewis, and Luca, 1967). The different art themes created by school-age boys and girls are therefore likely to reflect various socialization agents. During the school years, gender issues related to the peer group become intensified, as the peer group becomes an increasingly important socializing agent. Children enter a school system and spend large amounts of time with peers, whose opinions and behaviors take on greater importance (Berndt, 1979; Cromer, Ellis, and Rogoff, 1981; D'Andrea, 1983). Middle childhood is the peak age for conformity and adherence to the peer group's behavioral norms, and thus the peer group may also be a powerful influence on children's artistic behavior.

Gender segregation is highest during middle childhood (for example, Etaugh and Liss, 1992). Gender-segregated peer groups serve as powerful socialization environments through the amplification and extension of pre-existing sex differences (Maccoby, 1990; Maccoby and Jacklin, 1987; Thorne and Luria, 1986). Because children behave differently in a group than when they are alone (Maccoby and Jacklin, 1987), it is significant that gender segregation and own-sex favoritism is a robust feature of social relations during the school years (Maccoby, 1988, 1990; Powlishta, 1995). If middle childhood is a time when both conformity and same-sex segregation are at their highest, then one should expect that the influence of same-sex peers on children's art might be especially strong.

Middle childhood is also a time when a conformist stage of ego development emerges; children become conscious of their reputation, appearance, and status (Ferrara, 1991). This could explain children's adherence to gender norms in middle childhood, as well as why children manifest self-consciousness in their artwork and criticize others' work (Cunningham, 1997; Ferrara, 1991). Thus if children are self-conscious about their own work and critical of others' work, peers may influence each other's drawings.

Processes in Peer Collaborations

Such peer influence could occur through various means. Children's actual drawings—their themes, details, colors, or technical qualities—could function as models, offering children opportunities for observational learning. Observational learning has been posited as a crucial mechanism in children's learning in peer and collaborative contexts (for example, Botvin and Murray, 1975; Gauvain and Rogoff, 1989). Such learning would occur to the extent that children actually look at their peers' art, perhaps due to peers showing and displaying their work to others. In their conversations, children could share ideas and make explicit comparisons between each other's drawings and drawing techniques. Such exchanges would include many ability comparisons that could trigger artistic changes in children, particularly by motivating them to improve their drawings to bring them more in line with local norms of style (that is, the themes, technical qualities, and meanings in their peers' drawings).

Another component of conversation could be the evaluation of each other's drawings on various criteria. Such evaluations could provide encouragement or discouragement. One study of seven-year-olds found that children usually offer positive remarks about peers' art and often remark on its neatness (Cunningham, 1997). We might expect that in an older sample (as in this study's fifth-grade classroom), negative remarks are common, in part due to the stringent standards of literal and realistic drawings at this age (Gardner, 1980). Thus there seems to be ample room for peer criticism and conflict to be conveyed through verbal exchanges about the children's drawings; many sociocognitive processes appear to transmit peer influence on children's art.

Motivated by the rise of Vygotskian models of learning and development and guided participation (Vygotsky, 1978; Rogoff, 1990), there has been a great deal of investigation of collaborative learning in a peer context. For example, Duran and Gauvain (1993) found that in a joint planning task in which children had to devise sequential movements to deliver materials, novices benefited from having an expert partner who engaged them in the task. Of the different sociocognitive processes they studied, only guided participation with an expert peer, not conflict or observational learning, seemed to advance children's learning. Other studies of peer collaboration indicate that the level of peers' expertise influences children's learning and higher-level thinking (for example, Azmitia, 1988; Radziszewska and Rogoff, 1988). Having a partner with greater skill seems to benefit children, but not if the expert partner dominates discussion, ignores the peer, or does not offer clarifying comments. Another study of collaborative learning (Teasley, 1995) shows that in a computer-based reasoning task, simply having a peer partner does not promote children's learning, but learning is enhanced when children engage in dialogue with explanation, negotiation, and clarification. Thus a sociocognitive coordination between peers seems crucial for helping a partner advance in thinking and learning.

In our study we observe some of these peer processes in a naturalistic setting—processes that may influence school children's drawing. Given the emphasis on graphic realism during the school years, we expected to hear our fifth graders sharing many evaluative remarks and criticisms about their drawings. It may be the case that an ample portion of peer commentary is this kind of negative, external feedback. Such feedback may promote children's artistic development (Karmiloff-Smith, 1999).

The descriptive study here analyzed these kinds of mechanisms of peer influences on children's drawings. Fifth graders were naturalistically observed during a drawing session in their classroom. This age group was chosen because of its proficiency in linguistic and artistic skill, as well as its presumed concerns with conformity to peer norms. The observation of collaborative exchange in group drawing sessions could enhance our understanding of peers' influence on children's artistic styles.

Children's Sample and Setting

I (Chris Boyatzis) observed a fifth-grade class with twenty children in a small suburb of Boston in a drawing session that lasted about forty-five minutes. The teacher (Gretchen Albertini) distributed drawing materials to the tables. Such small-group activities were common in the class. Students were told they could sit with whomever they wished at any classroom table; each seated four to eight children.

Children grouped themselves quickly and rigidly along gender lines: boys sat with boys, girls with girls, with no instances of gender integration. The groups ranged in size from pairs sitting closely to one another to larger groups of three to five children drawing and speaking together. In some cases, larger groups of children at one table seemed to divide into pairs, often as a function of the theme of the particular children's drawings. I had often visited the class and was familiar to the children; I sat at different places in the room to observe the groups and record pertinent remarks and conversations about the artwork. Occasionally I spoke with the children about their art, but typically I remained in the background, trying to be as unobtrusive as possible. Children allowed me to collect the drawings at the end of the session.

Because the children grouped themselves along gender-segregated lines, we organized their drawings and conversations along gender lines as well, so we could then offer some conclusions about peer processes in drawing.

Boys' Drawings and Conversations

The children's drawings manifested a striking conformity to gender stereotypes, corroborating a gender difference that was evident in prior studies. Virtually all the boys drew violent or competitive scenes in sports or high-tech scenarios. The boys' drawings (presented shown in Figures 2.1, 2.2, 2.3, and 2.4) depict RoboCop-type figures and jet fighters engaged in combat. All of these pictures are drawn in pencil, devoid of color, and marked by precise angular, geometric shapes. The pictures reveal a thematic and technical conformity to peers' drawings.

During the drawing session, several boys and the teacher said that Jon, the boy who drew Figure 2.1, was recognized as the premiere artist in the class. His remarkably accurate and detailed rendition of a RoboCop character, common in violent and popular movies at that time, reflects his ability to draw referents in highly realistic ways, which may explain Jon's high artistic status. Jon had earned the position of expert, and his expertise manifested itself in at least two ways that are relevant to peer influence. First, he immediately announced to the group what his topic would be and began drawing without hesitation. His drawing served as a model and inspiration for another boy, Martin, who was seated next to Jon at the same table where a group of boys were drawing. Jon and Martin devoted their entire forty-five-minute

Figure 2.1. Drawing by Jon, Fifth-Grade Boy

drawing session to their RoboCop figures. Martin's drawing, shown in Figure 2.2, shows that he did not attempt to draw the complete RoboCop figure (the one that Jon was masterfully drawing) but is actually a study of a portion of the referent.

During the drawing session, Martin made many remarks that reflected a deferential respect for Jon. In one exchange, Martin was drawing and said to Jon, "Don't Robotechs and Varitechs transform?" Jon's reply, in a condescending tone, was "Varitech *means* transformable." During their drawing session, neither Jon nor Martin asked each other many questions about their drawings, but they did offer a running commentary on their own skills and difficulties in achieving their desired image. The following group discussion conveys the boys' frustrations in transferring a mental image to paper:

JON (drawing Figure 2.1): I don't think I'm good.
OBSERVER: Why?
JON: I think it looks wrong.
MARTIN (drawing Figure 2.2): I have this perfect picture in my head, but it comes out lousy!
MAX (drawing Figure 2.3): There's this clear image in my head, but it doesn't come out.
JON: I *can't draw humans*! Anything else, but *not* humans!

Figure 2.2. Drawing by Martin, Fifth-Grade Boy

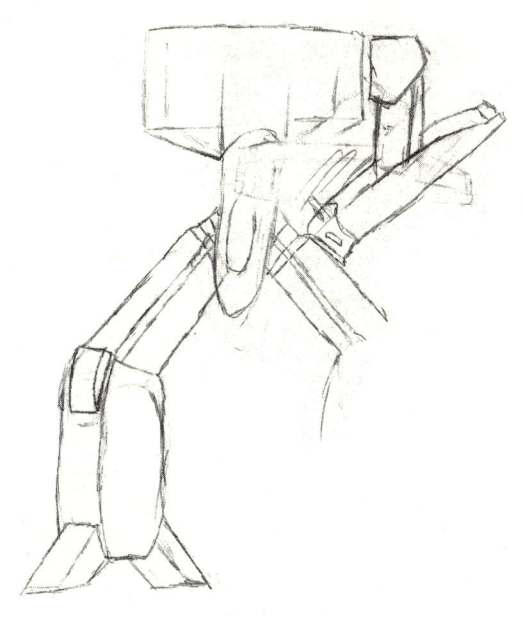

It is impossible to know whether Jon, the esteemed artist in the group, set off a chain reaction with his initial self-criticism. But all of the children's comments display a deep self-consciousness about their artistic skills—a self-criticism that stems from their perceived inability to draw the referents with a realistic and literal isomorphic correspondence to the actual entities.

The boys' final remarks further reflect the high expectations these realistic artists placed on themselves. Rising to turn in his drawing (Figure 2.1), Jon said in a self-deprecating tone, "Well, I'm missing an arm here. This is going to be pretty pathetic because I didn't have enough time." As he slid his drawing across the table, he shook his head in self-disgust and said, "I've done better." Shortly afterward, Martin handed his picture in and said, "Mine's pathetic, too." After forty-five minutes of intense drawing, these children influenced the evaluation of their own artwork.

Two other boys, drawing next to each other at the same large table where Jon and Martin sat, created Figures 2.3 and 2.4, with fighter-plane dogfights among three planes, resulting in the destruction of one plane and in missiles being en route to another.

Max drew Figure 2.3. Another boy at the table, Alex, expressed frustration with his inability to draw pictures and did not begin drawing until ten minutes into the session. Alex spoke of several interests, including sports, but admitted he could not draw any of them well. His self-consciousness was harmed by looking at his peers' drawings, including the proficiently drawn RoboCops, a social comparison that only seemed to impede Alex's desire to put pencil to paper. While drawing his fighter-plane action, Max offered

Figure 2.3. Drawing by Max, Fifth-Grade Boy

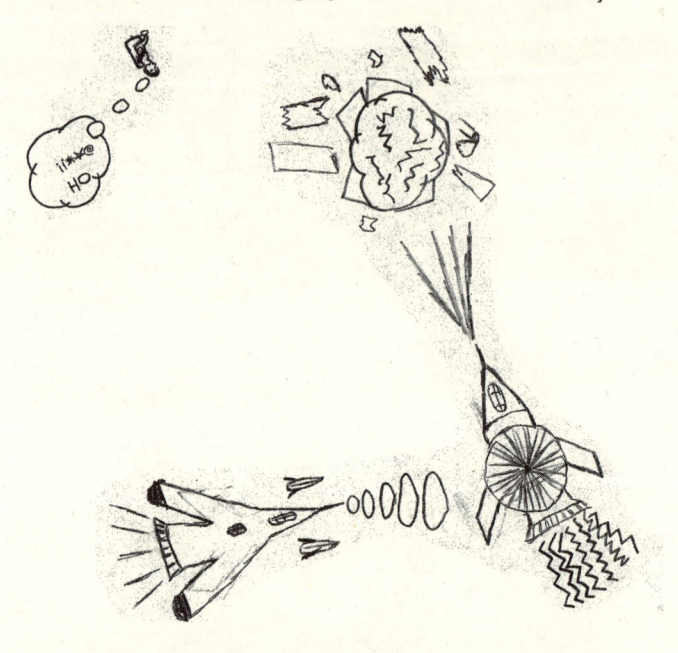

Figure 2.4. Drawing by Alex, Fifth-Grade Boy

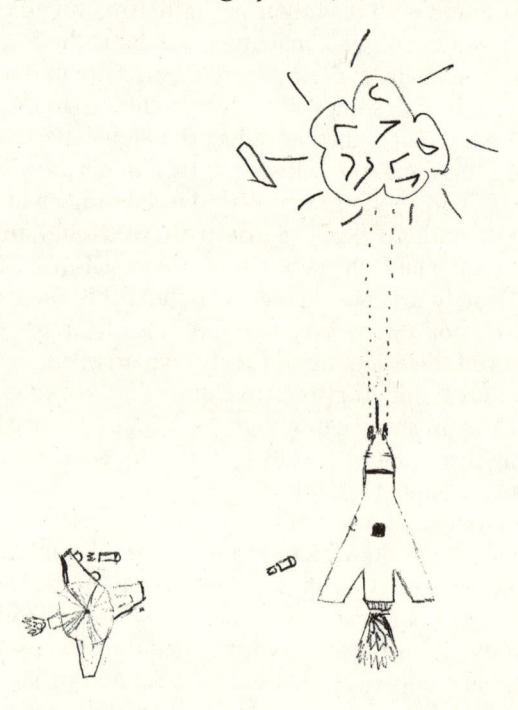

many self-criticisms. A few minutes into his drawing, he said, "I just tried to draw a fighter plane, but it sucks." Moments later, he said, "I tried to draw a fighter plane like this, but it was wrong." At this point, from across the table Jon raised his head, looked briefly at one of Max's planes, and yelled, "You're missing a tail!" This unsolicited evaluation by Jon, the expert peer, prompted all the boys at the table to suddenly direct their gaze to Max's paper, watching for his graphic solution. Because of either the specific criticism by Jon or the broader group pressure to do something, Max erased one of the planes in his drawing and began an improved version. Shortly after this, Alex finally began to draw and created Figure 2.4, an obvious copy of what Max was drawing right next to him. As in Jon's and Martin's pictures (Figures 2.1 and 2.2), the pictures by Max and Alex are strikingly similar in theme and technical detail.

During his drawing, Alex offered ongoing criticisms of his own work, often saying things like, "I have no idea if this is any good." At one point, while drawing one of the planes in his picture, he sheepishly asked Martin, "Is this any good? Is this a good plane?" This solicitation of evaluative feedback led to a gentle, "Yeah, it's OK," spoken in a positive tone. Some of the boys' verbal rounds were made without any cessation in their drawing; they did not even take their eyes from their drawings. These conversations seemed to have as their simple goal the exchange of information about the themes of the pictures. For example, at one point Alex asked, "Don't Apache helicopters shoot missiles?" Martin responded, "They have missile pods in their wings." Jon then offered, "They shoot eight laser missiles. I know what laser-targeted is, but not what laser-guided means." Periods of silence followed this conversation and other exchanges like them in which the boys shared information about their subject matter.

In sum, the boys' drawing session revealed strong conformity to each other's styles in subject matter, technical form, and meaning (Somerville, 1983). The verbal exchanges entailed ample self-criticisms, ongoing commentary about the drawing process, and both unsolicited and solicited evaluations from peers.

Girls' Drawings and Conversations

Several groups of three or four girls drew together; the girls were seated around large tables. The girls' groups displayed many of the conversational qualities in the boys' groups, despite a striking difference in thematic preference and style. The girls' themes consisted of nature, animals, and people. Several drawings by girls are presented in Figures 2.5, 2.6, 2.7, and 2.8. The technical qualities of the drawings are as different from the boys' drawings as the themes. The girls' drawings are largely organic forms, drawn with markers, crayons, and pens in different colors. For example, one girl drew a flower in vibrant color, prompting her peers to note its similarity to the Georgia O'Keeffe pictures the class had studied that week. The children were asked what they liked

Figure 2.5. Drawing by Chrissy, Fifth-Grade Girl

about the O'Keeffe pictures they studied, as well as their friend's drawing at the table. Most girls commented on the vibrant colors, but one girl, as if to show off her aesthetic vocabulary, looked at the O'Keeffe copy and said, "I like its . . . texture." There was a long pause at the table as everyone seemed to take in this astute reflection. Then suddenly the group laughed and mocked, "Its *texture*?!" When the girl was asked what she meant by texture, she giggled and admitted, "I don't know." This conversation, like many of the boys' exchanges, shows the peer group to be a mutual collaborative system in which ongoing commentary is offered on the themes and technicalities of the drawings.

Another girl at the table drew several personified and colorful suns, with sunglasses and smiles. As she drew them, she remarked that one wasn't as good as the other and explained that in the "bad" version "the smile isn't as good, and the sunglasses aren't as straight." Valerie spent the session drawing a woman in frontal view. The drawing was elaborate and detailed, with careful facial details and numerous sexual markers (jewelry, a tapered waist, breasts). At different points, the girls at the table offered unsolicited evaluations. One girl blurted, "The head's flat!" and another girl exhorted, "Make her have elbows!" One girl, Sally, was more careful, saying, "Your hair—it's always straight on top; then it goes *straight* down." Valerie's responses to this string of unsolicited criticisms indicated that such remarks helped her become aware of the shortcomings but she was not quite sure how to rectify them.

Figure 2.6. Drawing by Kristin, Fifty-Grade Girl

Sally seemed to have expert-artist status among her girl peers similar to Jon's status among his boy peers. Sally drew a picture on a large posterboard, depicting horses with riders jumping over gates. While drawing, Sally remarked, "I draw horses, and I have lots of animals—four horses." One interesting feature of Sally's drawing was that although she drew constantly throughout the forty-five minute session, at the twenty-minute point she had nothing on the poster. Her reach toward realism and her preoccupation with horses (see Gardner, 1980) led her to erase her drawings continuously until she felt that she had reached an acceptable degree of literalism. As she drew, Sally volunteered, "I like pencil. In case I mess up, I can erase." Upon hearing this self-consciousness, another girl looked at Sally's picture and said, "Sally, that is so good," to which Sally retorted, "No it's not!"

Figure 2.7. Drawing by Erin, Fifth-Grade Girl

During the session, the girls openly spoke of their artistic interests, and in so doing conveyed both their gender-related thematic preferences and their concern with realistic depiction. One girl said, "I usually draw flowers, sometimes houses." When asked if she draws other things, she replied, "Yeah, but I'm not good at them." Deirdre said she liked to draw cats, at which point another girl, Erin, said "I got rabbits this week." Asked if she ever draws them, she said, "No, I can't draw them well." In a different pairing of friends seated next to each other, Kristin was beginning to draw Figure 2.6 when her friend Chrissy asked, "Is that a globe?" Kristin replied, "Well, it's supposed to be."

Chrissy and Kristin drew Figures 2.5 and 2.6, respectively. Their thematic and technical similarities are obvious. Both girls were concerned with environmental well-being. This concern transcended their art. During their drawing, the girls were speaking when one stopped drawing and uttered, "Oh my God. I had tuna for lunch today!" The other, looking up from her picture, quickly checked, "Was it dolphin-safe?" Upon assuring herself and her friend that it was, the two returned to their drawings. As with the other girls (as well as the boys), their drawings reflected their ongoing concerns and interests.

Figures 2.7 and 2.8, by Erin and Deirdre, respectively, reflect another natural and organic theme. Erin began to draw her picture of the "female fat cat" in a natural setting with sun, clouds, and grass, and Deirdre soon began to work on her drawing of a cat.

Figure 2.8. Drawing by Deirdre, Fifth-Grade Girl

Two other girls, sitting close to each other and trying to draw people, shared this exchange:

ROBIN (drawing a face): I can't even draw eyes.
ANDREA (drawing a person): It's easy. You draw two circles . . . (shows Robin her drawing)
ROBIN (beginning to draw): Oh. (eyes on Andrea)
ANDREA: No, make the circle bigger. (Robin adjusts her circle.) Yea, better; well, I'm at a bad angle to really see.
ROBIN: I don't know if this is a good eye. Is this a good eye or not?
ANDREA: It's OK.

Conclusion

The children's art reveals a deep conformity to peers' thematic preferences and technical styles, as well as to broader gender stereotypes in art. The art also reflects a concern with getting their pictures "right," that is, as realistic and literal as possible. These findings are consistent with prior reports of gender differences that are in accord with gender stereotypes in school children's art (Cox, 1993; Feinburg, 1977; McNiff, 1982; Reeves and Boyette, 1983; Rubenstein and Rubin, 1984).

Although we did not quantify the sociocognitive processes at work in the children's drawing groups nor systematically assess their impact on children's drawing, this observation nevertheless offers rich information from a natural, ecologically valid situation on peer processes in a domain—children's art—that has been ignored by peer collaboration researchers and studied insufficiently by art researchers. Children's group drawing sessions can now be added to the range of contexts assessed in peer collaboration research on such topics as spatial tasks, errand planning, conservation problems, and mathematical balance beam tasks. An innovative finding from this naturalistic observation is that peers provide multiple forms of mutual influence on artwork, primarily through verbal communication during their drawing sessions.

Children spoke frequently, sharing solicited and unsolicited evaluations about each other's drawings. They gave extensive feedback to each other about technical qualities in the drawings and about realistic depictions of the referents ("You're missing a tail!" or "The head's flat!"). The comments to each other and the children's ongoing self-critical judgments while drawing provide evidence of rampant concern with the realistic depiction of referents, whether persons, animals, or military vehicles, as others have reported (for example, Cunningham, 1997; Gardner, 1980; Machotka, 1966). However, children rarely commented on neatness or color in their drawings, contrary to earlier findings of evaluative remarks of peers' art (Cunningham, 1997; Feinburg, 1977). It may be the case that children's concern with realism—with getting it right—subsumes more detailed issues of neatness or color.

One goal of the naturalistic observation was to identify the interpersonal dynamics of peer influence. The drawings themselves provide ample evidence of children copying their peers' themes and technical qualities. Copying peers' art (which itself often reflects more distal, culturally available graphic representations such as the RoboCop character) is a common feature in this age range (see, for example, Duncum, 1988; Gardner, 1980). So copying is one form of peer influence on children's artistic style, to the extent that children are at least inspired by or directly imitate a peer's thematic content, technical features, and meaning.

However, with our focus on verbal interaction in the drawing groups, we were struck by the substantial amount of discussion about the children's own and their peers' artwork. At a basic level, the occurrence of verbal communication between peers is likely to have helped the children understand their drawings better and draw pictures that are more acceptable to themselves and their peers (Berk, 1992; Teasley, 1995).

But it is clear from the research on peer collaboration that the *quality* of communication between peers, not just the occurrence of talk, is the crucial dynamic. In our observation, one category of comments was unsolicited evaluations by peers. This category, a common one, was illustrated by remarks such as Jon's critique of Max's fighter jet ("You're missing a tail!") and, with reference to Valerie's drawing of a woman, one girl's charge to "make her have elbows!" Though not analyzed systematically here, it seems that such negative feedback often led to a revision in the recipient's picture, as Karmiloff-Smith (1999) suggests could happen in response to such a critique. It is possible that the familiarity and friendship between these classmates created an interpersonal context in which uninvited criticisms were taken as genuine attempts to help the artist (and in all cases to make the drawing a more realistic and literal symbol of the referent). This personal closeness might facilitate intersubjectivity between peers, that is, the arriving at a more shared understanding through communication—a process that is crucial in Vygotskian models of learning (for example, Tudge, 1992). It is also possible that the children who were viewed as the class experts (Jon and Sally) may have offered verbal input or actual graphic models of their art that were particularly persuasive to their less skilled peers (Azmitia, 1988). Having an advanced partner is important for peer influence, but most evidence shows that the *quality* of the interaction and feedback from such a partner is crucial (Gauvain and Rogoff, 1989; Radziszewska and Rogoff, 1988; Teasley, 1995; Tudge, 1992). When the advanced partner offers feedback that carefully explains and clarifies, other children are more likely to benefit. It is also likely that children will benefit when peers not only verbalize ideas or solutions but offer each other actual models of alternative solutions and, as we saw in this study, show each other different ways of drawing referents (Azmitia, 1988; Duran and Gauvain, 1993).

One kind of utterance was the request for evaluation from a child struggling with his or her own picture (for example, Robin's request for Andrea's help ("Was this a good eye or not?") and Alex's question to Martin ("Is this a good plane?"). Some requests were for technical guidance, such as Robin's question to Andrea ("How do you draw eyes?"). The peer's response to such requests for evaluation represents another form of peer influence by providing discouragement or encouragement, as in Andrea's evaluation, "It's OK," and Martin's gentle approval of Alex's fighter plane. The peer's willingness to offer technical help also seems to be a form of peer influence, as in Andrea's modeling of how to draw eyes ("You draw two circles . . . no, make the circle bigger"). Specific evaluative feedback and the sharing of drawings occurred in the drawing sessions, and though there was no direct measure of improvement or artistic development in the observations, in many instances children revised and improved their drawings due to specific peer feedback and the sharing of actual drawing models.

In sum, the drawing sessions created a context of mutual and bilateral peer process. This image of artistic development as socially embedded is consistent with a Vygotskian model of development rather than one that characterizes the child as a solitary graphic problem solver. (It is curious that though Vygotsky discusses children's drawing in *Mind in Society* [1978; see pp. 112–114], he focuses on symbolic development and the relation between art and speech rather than the social processes that could influence such development.) Children surely draw alone, make stylistic choices independently, and undergo endogenous symbolic developments. But our observations and those in Chapters One and Five of this volume point toward the value of conceptualizing children's drawing and artistic development as occurring within sociocognitive contexts that may function as a zone of proximal development in which the interpsychological is internalized. In some cases the co-constructor may be an adult (a parent, teacher, art instructor) or peers. Surely children often draw alone, but even then they may benefit from hearing the internalized questions, evaluations, and suggestions of peers echoing from actual dyadic or group interaction. Researchers must study the co-construction of artwork to better understand both artistic development and peer collaboration. Future work should systematically assess children's drawing behavior with and without peer collaborators, and with peers of varying degrees of expertise. It may also be valuable to assess children's drawing behavior and running self-commentary during the drawing process both before and after collaborating with peers in drawing sessions; such a design may tell us if and how the interpsychological becomes the intrapsychological.

Of course, the exciting accomplishment of peer collaboration work over the past two decades is the analysis of particular dynamics and processes that affect children's performance, learning, and development. In our observations of these fifth-grade children, many kinds of conversational features functioned as mechanisms of peer influence on children's art, and these require more systematic study to understand the sociocognitive processes in peers' collaborative artwork. Such assessment will help us further understand how social processes in peer collaboration constrain and facilitate artistic development.

References

Azmitia, M. "Peer Interaction and Problem Solving: When Are Two Heads Better Than One?" *Child Development,* 1988, *59,* 87–96.
Basow, S. A. *Gender Stereotypes and Roles.* (3rd ed.) Pacific Grove, Calif.: Brooks/Cole, 1992.
Berk, L. E. "Children's Private Speech: An Overview of Theory and the Status of Research." In R. M. Diaz and L. E. Berk (eds.), *Private Speech: From Social Interaction to Self Regulation.* Mahwah, N.J.: Erlbaum, 1992.
Berndt, T. "Developmental Changes in Conformity to Peers and Parents." *Developmental Psychology,* 1979, *15,* 608–616.
Block, J. H. *Sex-Role Identity and Ego Development.* San Francisco: Jossey-Bass, 1984.
Botvin, G. J., and Murray, F. B. "The Efficacy of Peer Modeling and Social Conflict in the Acquisition of Conservation." *Child Development,* 1975, *46,* 796–799.
Boyatzis, C. J., and Eades, J. "Gender Differences in Preschoolers' and Kindergartners' Artistic Production and Preference." *Sex Roles,* 1999, *41,* 627–638.
Boyatzis, C. J., and Parisella, J. "Do Artistic Sex Differences Emerge as Early as the Preschool Years? Home Environment and Cognitive Correlates of Sex Differences in Scribblers." Unpublished manuscript, 2000.
Cox, M. V. *Children's Drawings of the Human Figure.* Mahwah, N.J.: Erlbaum, 1993.
Cromer, C. C., Ellis, S., and Rogoff, B. "Age Segregation in Children's Social Interactions." *Developmental Psychology,* 1981, *17,* 399–407.
Cunningham, A. "Criteria and Processes Used by Seven-Year-Old Children in Appraising Art Work of their Peers." *Visual Arts Research,* 1997, *23,* 41–48.
D'Andrea, M. D. "Social Development During Middle Childhood: Clarifying Some Misconceptions." *Elementary School Guidance and School Counseling,* 1983, *17,* 214–220.
Duncum, P. "To Copy or Not to Copy: A Review." *Studies in Art Education,* 1988, *29,* 203–210.

Duran, R. T., and Gauvain, M. "The Role of Age Versus Expertise in Peer Collaboration During Joint Planning." *Journal of Experimental Child Psychology*, 1993, 55, 227–242.

Etaugh, C., and Liss, M. B. "Home, School, and Playroom: Training Grounds for Adult Gender Roles." *Sex Roles*, 1992, 26, 129–147.

Feinburg, S. "Conceptual Content and Spatial Characteristics in Boys' and Girls' Drawings of Fighting and Helping." *Studies in Art Education*, 1977, 18, 63–72.

Ferrara, N. "Art as a Reflection of Child Development." *American Journal of Art Therapy*, 1991, 30, 44–50.

Gardner, H. *Artful Scribbles: The Significance of Children's Drawings*. New York: Basic Books, 1980.

Gauvain, M., and Rogoff, B. "Collaborative Problem Solving and Children's Planning Skills." *Developmental Psychology*, 1989, 25, 139–151.

Karmiloff-Smith, A. "Taking Development Seriously." *Human Development*, 1999, 42, 325–327.

Kawecki, I. "Gender Differences in Young Children's Artwork." *British Educational Research Journal*, 1994, 20, 485–490.

Lange-Küttner, C., and Edelstein, W. "The Contribution of Social Factors to the Development of Graphic Competence." In C. Lange-Küttner and G. Thomas (eds.), *Drawing and Looking*. Hertfordshire, England: Harvester Wheatsheaf, 1995.

Lark-Horovitz, B., Lewis, H. P., and Luca, M. *Understanding Children's Art for Better Teaching*. Upper Saddle River, N.J.: Merrill, 1967.

Maccoby, E. E. "Gender as a Social Category." *Developmental Psychology*, 1988, 24, 755–765.

Maccoby, E. E. "Gender and Relationships: A Developmental Account." *American Psychologist*, 1990, 45, 513–520.

Maccoby, E. E., and Jacklin, C. N. "Gender Segregation in Childhood." In H. W. Reese (ed.), *Advances in Child Development and Behavior*. Orlando, Fla.: Academic Press, 1987.

Machotka, P. "Aesthetic Criteria in Childhood." *Child Development*, 1966, 37, 877–885.

Machover, K. "Sex Differences in the Developmental Pattern of Children as Seen in Human Figure Drawings." In A. I. Rabin and M. R. Haworth (eds.), *Projective Techniques with Children*. Philadelphia: Grune & Stratton, 1960.

McNiff, K. "Sex Differences in Children's Art." *Journal of Education*, 1982, 164, 271–289.

Pomerleau, A., Bolduc, D., Malcuit, G., and Cossette, L. "Pink or Blue: Environmental Gender Stereotypes in the First Two Years of Life." *Sex Roles*, 1990, 22, 359–367.

Powlishta, K. K. "Intergroup Processes in Childhood: Social Categorization and Sex Role Development." *Developmental Psychology*, 1995, 31, 781–788.

Radziszewska, B., and Rogoff, B. "Influence of Adult and Peer Collaborators on Children's Planning Skills." *Developmental Psychology*, 1988, 24, 840–848.

Reeves, J. B., and Boyette, N. "What Does Children's Artwork Tell Us About Gender?" *Qualitative Sociology*, 1983, 6, 322–333.

Rogoff, B. *Apprentices in Thinking*. New York: Oxford University Press, 1990.

Rubenstein, J., and Rubin, C. "Children's Fantasies of Interaction with Same and Opposite Sex Peers." In T. Field, J. Roopnarine, and M. Segal (eds.), *Friendship in Normal and Handicapped Children*. Norwood, N.J.: Ablex, 1984.

Somerville, S. C. "Individual Drawing Styles of Three Children from Five to Seven Years." In D. Rogers and J. A. Sloboda (eds.), *The Acquisition of Symbolic Skills*. New York: Plenum, 1983.

Teasley, S. D. "The Role of Talk in Children's Peer Collaborations." *Developmental Psychology*, 1995, 31, 207–220.

Thorne, B. "Girls and Boys Together . . . but Mostly Apart: Gender Arrangements in Elementary Schools." In W. W. Hartup and Z. Rubin (eds.), *Relationships and Development*. Mahwah, N.J.: Erlbaum, 1986.

Thorne, B. *Gender Play: Girls and Boys in School*. New Brunswick, N.J.: Rutgers University Press, 1993.

Thorne, B., and Luria, Z. "Sexuality and Gender in Children's Daily Worlds." *Social Problems*, 1986, *13*, 176–190.

Tudge, J.R.H. "Processes and Consequences of Peer Collaboration: A Vygotskian Analysis." *Child Development*, 1992, *63*, 1364–1379.

Vygotsky, L. S. *Mind in Society*. Cambridge, Mass.: Harvard University Press, 1978.

CHRIS J. BOYATZIS *is associate professor of psychology at Bucknell University, where his primary research interests are children's artistic development and religious and spiritual development.*

GRETCHEN ALBERTINI *teaches third grade at the Edward Devotion School in Brookline, Massachusetts.*

Adult judges assessed the distinctiveness of individual drawing styles of three- to ten-year-old children and found that about one-third of the children had distinctive styles. These children were found most frequently in the younger age groups and showed higher aesthetic appeal and creativity ratings in their drawings than children who did not have distinctive styles.

The Development of Individual Styles in Children's Drawing

Malcolm W. Watson, Susan Nozyce Schwartz

The questions of when a distinctive style in art production emerges and how it develops are important not only for what we can learn about human development generally but for what we can learn about the specific nature of aesthetic skills (Wieder, 1998). For example, is the possession of a distinctive style a prerequisite for a person's artwork being deemed aesthetic and deserving of the label "good art"? Gardner (1980) believes that for individuals to be labeled good artists they must not simply possess distinctive styles but must demonstrate a level of control that allows them to regulate their styles and the intention to create a specific product. In this view, a young child's work might show aesthetic and creative qualities, but these qualities would be viewed as accidental by-products of the child's art production. The child would not be deemed a good artist capable of producing truly aesthetic works until she demonstrated the intention to create a certain effect and had enough control of her style to do so. Gardner thought this capability did not truly develop until adolescence.

Yet there is no consensus as to whether the possession of aesthetic quality and aesthetic intent is necessary for a child to have an individual art style. For example, Kellogg (1970) argues that intentional aesthetic production is an integral part of artistic style, even though she found that adults could recognize individual art styles in children as young as four years of age, well before the children could be credited with aesthetic intent. This example illustrates the continuing confusion about the definition of artistic style and the necessary components for its emergence in young children.

In this chapter we first discuss some of the major issues and confusions surrounding the definition and assessment of individual styles in children's drawing and art. We then describe our study of the emergence of individual styles and conclude with a discussion of the probable sequence in children's development of artistic style.

Definition of Style

Somerville (1983) believes that artistic style comprises three major components: (1) the form (or qualities and techniques of the artist), (2) the subject matter (or content), and (3) the intended meaning (or purpose of the artist). Others have argued that neither subject matter nor the artist's intended meaning is necessary to define an individual style.

In their study of the artwork of four- to ten-year-olds, Pufall, Parker, and Falck (1982) define artistic style as "that perceivable quality of drawings which differentiates artists even when they are drawing the same content; and, moreover, that is sustained in artists' work even as content varies" (p. 3). This definition assumes that style can be discerned and that it is independent of the subject matter of the artwork. They found that adult judges could accurately identify which child did a particular drawing, even when content varies and regardless of whether the judges could identify the content. (In a similar vein, Boyatzis and Eades, 1999, found that judges could discriminate sex differences in style even when four-year-olds produced nothing but scribbles.) Yet Pufall and Pesonen (see Chapter Five) define style by both the formal properties of the work and the work's content and intention. For them, style is a combination of the *how* and the *what* of a person's artwork. Thus researchers are not consistent, even with themselves, in their conceptions of what comprises style.

In determining the role of content and intention in defining style, one must realize that an artist's techniques and qualities of drawing and painting will be influenced by the content and intended meaning of the artwork just as surely as they are influenced by the particular medium (Smith, 1979). Just as form and function are intertwined in the development of children's symbolic object use in play (Jackowitz and Watson, 1980), form, medium, and content are intertwined in art production and in the development of one's style.

Identifying the Components of Style

Behind every definition of artistic style is a common assumption that the style of one artist can be compared to and distinguished from the style of another artist. The definition we use in our study assumes that an individual style is based on components and qualities that are common across the artworks of the same artist and yet are distinctive from the components and qualities found in the artworks of other artists. When comparing works of art, a judge may not be able to identify explicitly the specific components that make one person's style distinctive from another's but still be able to distinguish one artist's work from another. In such cases we would say that the artist has a distinctive style, although further research would be required to identify which components were used implicitly by judges to differentiate one artist from another.

Researchers conclude that an individual, distinctive style is present when adult judges are able to say that two or more artworks are done by the same child artist (a match) and can correctly identify matches at better than chance levels (Gandini and Pufall, 1985; Pufall, Parker, and Falck, 1982; see also Chapter Four).

Hartley, Somerville, Jensen, and Eliefja (1982) and Somerville (1983) first trained adults to recognize the artworks of individual children and then determined whether these individuals could identify matches of subsequent drawings with the earlier drawings. Their judges could not correctly match drawings until they had first been trained to recognize a child's body of artwork. These researchers concluded that a distinctive style was present when judges could correctly match drawings done by the same artist, even though these judges could not necessarily identify the specific components that determined the children's distinctive styles or even say which components they used to make their judgments.

To complicate matters further, some artists may show distinctiveness in one component (for example, color saturation or boldness of line), whereas others show this distinctiveness in different components; these distinctions may or may not remain stable across the individual artist's development. Gandini and Pufall (1985) assessed the emergence of distinctive features in the drawings of five three-year-olds over several months. The children differed in the components or qualities that remained stable and made their artwork distinctive across time. Although these young participants did not have the ability to depict referents in a way that adults could easily identify, one child's artworks, for example, could be recognized because he consistently used checkered patterns; another child consistently used concentric circles. Each child who displayed a distinctive style showed it through different qualities or components.

To complicate matters even further, distinctiveness may be evident in the works of some young artists and not in others of the same age. For example, Somerville (1983) found that only two-thirds of her young artists had artistic styles that could be identified above chance levels.

Consensual Assessment

Despite the unanswered questions regarding the components of distinctive style, the extant research supports our simple definition. We claim that distinctive style is present when artworks can be discriminated. This definition falls under the rubric of a consensual assessment technique used to operationally define constructs that are difficult to elucidate, even though judges know the construct when they see it. Hennessey and Amabile (1999) have reasoned that if a group of observers agree (or form a consensus) that a product has a certain quality (in this case a distinctive style or a match with other products), even though they had not been given an explicit set of defining features, then that quality is said to be present. All that is needed is that some high degree of inter-judge reliability be reached.

Although this consensual assessment technique has been used to define operationally various abstract constructs, it does not provide much information about which components determine a particular construct (for example, in Hennessey and Amabile's research it was the construct of creativity; in our study, the construct of individual artistic style). Even if we know that distinctive, discernible styles exist in a group of children, we still may not understand what makes one style different from another. Once artistic style has been identified, further assessment of the artwork is needed to elucidate which components and qualities are crucial in determining individual styles. Thus to determine whether a distinctive style exists for an artist and when it emerges calls for a different assessment procedure than to determine what comprises a distinctive style. In the present study, our procedure was to have adult judges rate a number of components (for example, boldness of line, coverage of the surface) independent of judgments of distinctiveness of style and then assess whether these various ratings of components correlated with accuracy of identification of the individual styles.

Developmental Sequence

In addition to an interest in the emergence of and composition of styles, most researchers of children's art hope to determine whether developmental sequences exist, whether certain developmental or environmental milestones are associated with shifts in style, and whether steps in a sequence are consistently tied to specific ages. What is the likely course of this development? It would seem that some minimal mastery of a medium, such as paper and pencils, is necessary before the glimmerings of a child's individual drawing style could emerge. Yet there is evidence that even in a child's initial scribbling, one child's style can be distinguished from another's, at least in differentiating male from female scribbles (Boyatzis and Eades, 1999). Although innate behavioral differences may play a role in individual styles even before a child includes symbol use in her drawing, once she begins using drawing and marking to symbolize referents and puts some effort into differentiating the various marks, the distinctiveness of that child's drawings would be expected to increase. As the older child puts increasing effort into making appropriate symbols and also tries to make the drawings more aesthetic and more creative, distinctiveness may increase further. Thus the initial emergence of a distinctive style may occur in the early preschool years, but its fruition may not come until adolescence or beyond.

Some researchers have questioned the effects of art training and children's attempts at imitating models (either peers, teachers, or master artists) on children's distinctiveness of style (for example, see Chapter Two). Gardner (1980) and others have argued that during middle childhood children become more obsessed with drawing the way their peers draw and, because of this slavish conformity, become less creative. They focus on making the referents for their graphic symbols easily identifiable by using standardized drawing techniques. Some argue that they are focusing on drawing realistically, but it appears to us that they are attempting to draw recognizable symbols, whether these symbols be stylized forms or highly realistic (see also Chapter Two). For example, children use a standard form for a house or a tree or a cloud. Thus their drawing styles become less distinctive, as well as less creative.

However, Gombrich (1969) argues that with increasing age and training in art, children would be encouraged by teachers, who in Western cultures have a penchant for creativity, to experiment with new styles. He believed that training is apt to bring about discontinuity and is likely to increase distinctiveness of the newly emerging individual styles. Pufall and others (1982) argue that adults could either encourage or discourage children to change their styles. In effect, teachers are likely to encourage certain preferred or accepted styles and discourage others. Thus this influence could cause discontinuity in drawing style and also development toward a more standardized, nondistinctive style in middle childhood and adolescence.

In a study of the stability of drawing styles across time, Van Sommers (1983) reports that, when given standard drawings to copy, five- to six-year-olds do not incorporate many of the components and techniques shown in the models. When children at this age make multiple drawings over many drawing sessions, they essentially retain their initial, visual schemas and distinctive qualities, even though they add new elements and practice variations on a given theme.

These findings reflect a process of development described by Siegler (1994), who found evidence that children use new strategies of problem solving in mathematics (as well as in other cognitive domains) in an intermittent manner rather than in an all-or-none shift. Typically, children employ a new and more efficient problem-solving strategy once or twice but for some period of time return to their original strategies; gradually, they use the new strategy more frequently until it dominates. Even at this point the earlier strategies of problem solving remain and are used occasionally. Shifts in drawing style may follow the same progression. Changes may be incorporated intermittently rather than on an all-or-none basis. The same basic qualities of a person's drawing style may appear off and on for a long period of time or be present throughout the person's life of drawing, even when shifts occur.

Method and Participants

To shed light on the issues and questions regarding the development of distinctive styles of drawing and art in children, we completed a study involving the drawings of preschool and elementary school–aged children. We attempted to answer two main questions: (1) Are there distinctive styles that can be identified in most young children, and when do they emerge? (2) For those children who have distinctive styles, which components distinguish one style from another?

Child artists were thirty-two children from middle-class neighborhoods who had no known health problems or developmental disabilities and who had had no art training beyond that experienced in their regular school classes. There were four girls and four boys in each of four grades: (1) preschoolers (three- to four-year-olds), (2) kindergartners (five- to six-year-olds), (3) second graders (seven- to eight-year-olds), and (4) fourth graders (nine- to ten-year-olds). We limited the number of artists to keep the number of drawings that judges were required to assess at a manageable level.

Adult judges consisted of twenty undergraduate students at a private New England university who were not majoring or minoring in art. There were approximately equal numbers of males and females, ranging in age from eighteen to twenty-two years.

Each child was asked to make drawings using five colors of Crayola magic markers on 8-by-11-inch pieces of white paper. These drawings were produced in the child's day-care center or school during special art classes over a period of several weeks. The child was asked to produce four specific drawings: (1) a free drawing—the artist's choice of content, (2) a person, (3) a dog, and (4) a house and tree. Each drawing was coded on the back so the investigators, but not the judges, could identify the artist. See Figures 3.1, 3.2, 3.3, and 3.4 for examples. Figures 3.1 and 3.2 are of a person and a dog drawn by a preschooler. Figures 3.3 and 3.4 are of a person and a dog drawn by a fourth grader.

There were 128 drawings used in the study (4 drawings by 32 child artists). To make the judging task more manageable, these drawings were divided into two sets of 64 drawings each so that each judge could complete his or her assessments in an individual, two-hour session, independent of other judges. Ten judges were randomly chosen to assess each set.

Each set of sixty-four drawings contained all four drawings from sixteen children (with two boys and two girls randomly chosen from each of the four age groups). Thus the two sets were expected to be comparable in characteristics.

Judges were first shown all sixty-four drawings so that they could become familiar with the entire set. Then they were asked to rate, on a 5-point Likert scale, each of the drawings (in any order they wished) for aesthetic appeal, however they defined it. After all drawings were rated, the judges were asked to make a second pass through the drawings and rate

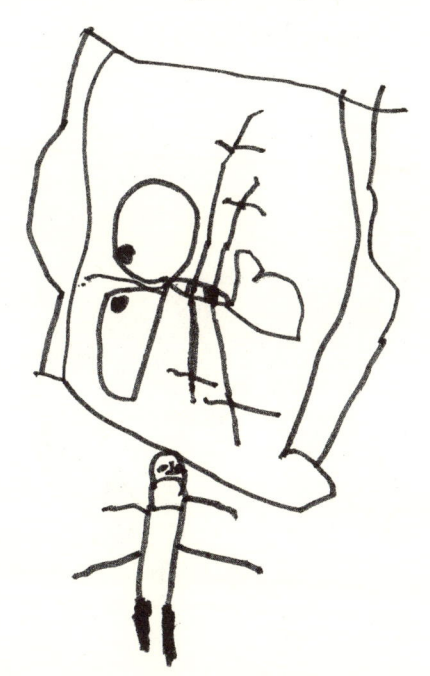

THE DEVELOPMENT OF INDIVIDUAL STYLES IN CHILDREN'S DRAWING 55

Figure 3.1. Drawing of a Person by a Preschooler

Figure 3.2. Drawing of a Dog by a Preschooler

Figure 3.3. Drawing of a Person by a Fourth Grader

Figure 3.4. Drawing of a Dog by a Fourth Grader

each one, again on a 5-point Likert scale, for creativity relative to the other drawings, however they defined it. The judges were now quite familiar with all the drawings.

After a break, sixteen of the sixty-four drawings, one from each child artist, were laid on a table. These prototypes were the free drawings with content of the child's choice. Judges were told that each drawing was completed by a different child and that three remaining drawings were done by each child. Judges were then asked to sort the remaining drawings so that the three drawings by each child were matched to each of the sixteen prototype drawings. This sorting task functioned like a Q-sort, and each judge had to use personal criteria to decide on the sorting. No further criteria or definitions of style or components were given.

Of course, the sortings for each artist were not independent of each other. If a judge inaccurately placed mismatched drawings into one pile, of necessity he or she would place mismatched drawings into other piles as well. Relative to other matching tasks that have been used, we considered this sorting task to be a conservative and relatively stringent procedure for assessing distinctive styles.

After all the drawings were sorted, judges completed a questionnaire regarding the individual criteria they had used in their sorting task. First, judges were asked to estimate the age and sex of the child artist for each of the sixteen piles of four drawings. Second, they were given the following list of seven components and asked to check which components they used in discriminating each artist. The components were (1) theme or topic, (2) geometric shapes or patterns present or absent, (3) placement of drawings on the page, (4) colors used, (5) type and quality of line, (6) unification or fragmentation of drawings, and (7) technical ability. In addition, judges were asked to list any other component they used. Only "degree of saturation of color" was mentioned more than once, and this quality was added as an eighth component.

Two scores were computed for the degree of accuracy in making correct matches of the drawings. First, the number of accurately matched drawings (that is, drawings sorted together that were indeed done by the same child artist) were noted for each child artist for each of the ten judges. Thus each artist could receive a 1 (which meant that the prototype drawing stood alone with no other matched drawings), 2, 3, or 4 (which meant that all four drawings were placed together) from each judge. Second, each artist's distinctiveness score was coded by computing the number of judges out of ten who were able to place three or four of his or her drawings together. This was a more stringent criterion of distinctiveness than the first score. The artists who reached the criterion of having at least 50 percent of the judges (five or more) place three or four of their drawings together were considered to be those with the most distinctive drawing styles. Some subsequent analyses were completed on this group of children separately. Two coders, independent of each other, each computed 75 percent of the coding scores and agreed on the 25 percent of the coding that they both completed.

Results and Discussion

In preliminary analyses, one-way analyses of variance (ANOVAs) were completed, with the two drawing sets of sixty-four drawings each as the independent variable and the various accuracy scores as the dependent variables. No significant main effects of drawing set were found; in subsequent analyses, the two sets of drawings were collapsed.

Judges predicted accurately the sex of the artist (ranging from 70 percent accuracy for preschoolers to 88 percent accuracy for fourth graders). Thus there was something about the content or stylistic components that generally differed in boys and girls, and these differences increased with increasing age. These results are consistent with the findings of Boyatzis and Eades (1999) in which judges could differentiate the drawings of boys and girls as young as four and one-half years of age, based on stylistic components in their drawings.

However, judges did not predict accurately the age of the artist except at the preschool level. Predictions of age ranged from 86 percent accuracy for preschoolers, declining to 31 percent for kindergartners, and declining further to a low of 22 percent for fourth graders. Thus judges were generally able to recognize when preschoolers did a drawing but were not able to differentiate the drawings in the older three age groups.

Emergence of a Distinctive Style

The first main question that we asked was whether distinctive styles can be identified in most young children and when they emerge. We found no overall age or sex differences in distinctiveness of individual style, as assessed by the judges' matchings. ANOVAs indicated no significant main effects of age or sex or interactions for the mean number of matched drawings that were found for each child across all ten judges. Neither were there significant age or sex effects for the mean number of judges who were able to match three or four drawings for each child—the more stringent criterion for distinctiveness.

We were primarily interested in whether there was a consensual agreement across judges on the distinctiveness of individual drawing styles. In general we did not find this consensual agreement. Across all judges for all picture sets, the combined inter-judge reliability was only .36. Considering the difficulty of the task of matching four drawings for each of sixteen children during one session, the lack of art training of the judges, and their initial lack of familiarity with the works of individual child artists, this low reliability is not surprising.

When we looked at distinctiveness ratings for individual children, we found that 34 percent (eleven of thirty-two children) showed a high level of distinctiveness as rated by judges (that is, at least five of ten judges matched three or four of their drawings). In preschoolers, 50 percent (four of eight children) reached this criterion; in kindergartners, 38 percent (three of eight children) reached it; in second graders, 38 percent (three of eight children) reached this criterion. Yet in fourth graders only 13 percent (one of eight children) reached this criterion, with all ten judges accurately matching all of this child's drawings. Thus, even though there was inconsistency in judgments of style at all ages, for the youngest three age groups 42 percent of the children had distinctive styles. This finding indicates that some components could indeed be discriminated and were consistent across a given child's drawings but different from the qualities in other children's drawings. By fourth grade, the children (except for the one child with consistently high distinctiveness ratings) were assumed not to have these distinctive features. These findings suggest that a standardization in drawing styles develops in middle childhood, and this standardization effects a decline in distinctiveness that had been present in many children beginning in the preschool years.

Components of a Distinctive Style

For children who have a distinctive style, which components distinguish one style from another? To answer this question we asked judges to identify the components they had used in making their judgments. Two-way ANOVAs showed no significant main effects of age or sex or interactions on the frequency of each component mentioned by the judges for the children's drawings. There were also low inter-judge reliabilities for the components mentioned by the different judges.

However, there was high inter-judge reliability on ratings for aesthetic appeal for each drawing, $r = .92$, and for creativity for each drawing, $r = .77$. Also aesthetic appeal and creativity ratings were highly correlated, $r = .78$. An Age × Sex ANOVA showed a main effect of age for mean aesthetic score for each drawing, $F(3,24) = 29.19$, $p < .0005$. Tukey post hoc analyses, with a $p < .05$ significance level, showed a significant increase in aesthetic appeal from preschoolers to kindergartners, but with a leveling off of scores by second grade. The mean aesthetic scores on the 5-point scale were 1.62 for preschoolers, 2.46 for kindergartners, 3.16 for second graders, and 3.14 for fourth graders. There was also a main effect of sex for mean aesthetic level of the drawings, $F(1,24)$ 8.62, $p < .01$, with girls ($m = 2.79$) having more aesthetic appeal than boys ($m = 2.40$).

An Age × Sex ANOVA also showed a main effect of age for mean creativity scores for each drawing, $F(3,24) = 30.10$, $p < .0005$. Tukey post hoc analyses showed a significant difference between preschoolers and second and fourth graders, with a leveling off of scores by kindergarten. The mean creativity scores on the 5-point scale were 1.92 for preschoolers, 2.50 for kindergartners, 2.89 for second graders, and 2.78 for fourth graders. There was no main effect of sex or interaction for mean creativity scores.

In summary, aesthetic appeal and creativity could be reliably assessed across the judges (that is, with judges showing consensual assessment) and showed increases with increasing age. Yet for none of the other components we assessed did judges' ratings show consistency or age changes across all children. No significant correlations of aesthetic appeal or creativity with the other eight components were found.

Although there was no consistency of components used for all children, there was some consistency for the eleven children who showed a high level of distinctive style, as judged by the criterion of having at least five judges match at least three or four drawings accurately. Table 3.1 gives the mean number of judges who mentioned using each of the eight components for these children. It also gives the mean ratings of aesthetic appeal and creativity for the same groups. For preschoolers, two components (use of geometric shapes and use of line) were mentioned as being important considerations by about five judges or more. For kindergartners, no component was mentioned by five or more judges. For second graders, two components were mentioned by about five judges. For the one child at the fourth-grade level, three components were mentioned by five or more judges, but the consensus of the judges was extremely high for this one child. His highly distinctive style seemed to depend on his distinctive use of colors, unified drawings, and high technical ability. In fact, use of colors, unified drawings, and technical abilities were the components most often mentioned by judges as being important in their judgments of children at all ages. (This occurred even in judges' analysis of preschoolers' scribbles in Boyatzis and Eades, 1999, and Boyatzis and Parisella, 2000.) Interestingly, for children at all ages, the theme of the drawings was never mentioned by five or more judges as being an important component. (Of course, in this study, the themes of most of the drawings by the children were mandated and thus controlled.) Also the components of color saturation, use of geometric shapes or patterns, and placement on the page were seldom mentioned by judges.

Aesthetic appeal and creativity were both rated higher in the eleven artists with distinctive styles than in the other twenty-one artists. As can be seen in Table 3.1, with increasing age these qualities of the eleven artists with highly distinctive styles also consistently increased.

Conclusions

These results show that a distinctive style in children's drawings does not emerge in all children at any age. Nevertheless, 34 percent of the children did indeed show a recognizable, distinctive style in their artworks, even as young as three and four years of age. Most studies using a consensual assessment technique (see Hennessey and Amabile, 1999) involve judges who have expertise in the domain they are assessing or have been trained to recognize specific artists' works (for example, Hartley and others, 1982;

Table 3.1. Components Used and Ratings for Twelve Children with Distinctive Styles

Component	Mean Number of Judges Using Components for Each Age Group			
	P	K	2	4
Theme	3.5	2.0	2.0	0.0
Shapes	4.8	2.3	3.5	3.0
Placement	2.5	3.0	4.8	3.0
Colors	2.5	3.7	4.3	10.0
Line quality	4.8	3.3	4.0	4.0
Unification	3.0	3.0	5.0	7.0
Technical ability	3.8	3.3	4.0	8.0
Saturation	0.3	0.7	1.3	0.0
	Mean Judges' Rating (on 5-point scale) for Each Age Group			
Aesthetic appeal	1.5	2.8	3.2	3.5
Creativity	1.8	2.5	2.9	3.3

Somerville, 1983). Our judges were young adults who were not trained in art or children's drawings and had no previous experience with the children's artworks, yet they could match drawings for approximately one-third of the child artists on a difficult sorting task. More experienced judges with a simpler matching task may have found even more distinctiveness in children's drawings.

Some of the components or qualities that we assessed seemed to be used as part of the judgments (for example, use of color and technical ability), but it isn't clear that we considered the qualities of children's artwork that most distinguish one from another. It was clear that, in general, the artists who had more distinctive styles also did drawings with higher ratings in technical ability, aesthetic appeal, and creativity than those children who had less distinctive styles. In other words, a child's possession of a distinctive style was based on more advanced drawing abilities.

In conclusion, based on previous research as well as the results of this study, we would propose the following general sequence of the development of drawing style. Individual styles may begin to emerge when children gain some mastery over a particular art medium, probably as young as three years of age. During the late preschool years, distinctiveness seems to increase as children attempt to incorporate more symbolism into their artworks and use art as a tool to depict certain referents and themes. During the middle childhood years (by fourth grade in our study), distinctiveness may increase for some children and decrease for many others when they pay more attention to the styles of their peers' art productions and to adult teachers and models (see Chapter Two; see also Flannery and Watson, 1991). During adolescence, distinctiveness may remain set at the middle childhood level for those who stop drawing, but it may increase and show a noticeable discontinuity for the few individuals who continue to draw and paint and who attempt to increase their drawing and painting skills (see Chapter Four). At this time in particular, some adolescent artists attempt to add more aesthetic and creative qualities to their artworks (Gardner, 1980). Thus there is no all-or-none process in the emergence of a distinctive style but rather a gradual development that may include periods of decreased distinctiveness and discontinuities in style when the child attempts changes or when major developmental milestones in other domains influence art production. There may be both a foundation style that develops early on and remains in the child's artwork and shifting qualities in some components at times of developmental or environmental change.

References

Boyatzis, C. J., and Eades, J. "Gender Differences in Preschoolers' and Kindergartners' Artistic Production and Preference." *Sex Roles,* 1999, *41,* 627–638.

Boyatzis, C. J., and Parisella, J. "Do Artistic Sex Differences Emerge as Early as the Preschool Years? Home Environment and Cognitive Correlates of Sex Differences in Scribblers." Unpublished manuscript, 2000.

Flannery, K. A., and Watson, M. W. "Perceived Competence in Drawing During the Middle Childhood Years." *Visual Arts Research,* 1991, *17,* 66–71.

Gandini, L., and Pufall, P. B. "Individual Style in Three-Year-Old Children's Painting." Paper presented at the meeting of the Jean Piaget Society, Philadelphia, June 1985.

Gardner, H. *Artful Scribbles: The Significance of Children's Drawings.* New York: Basic Books, 1980.

Gombrich, E. H. *Art and Illusion: A Study in the Psychology of Pictorial Representation.* Princeton, N.J.: Princeton University Press, 1969.

Hartley, J. L., Somerville, S. C., Jensen, D.V.C., and Eliefja, C. C. "Abstraction of Individual Styles from the Drawings of Five-Year-Old Children." *Child Development,* 1982, *53,* 1193–1214.

Hennessey, B. A., and Amabile, T. M. "Consensual Assessment." In M. A. Runco and S. R. Pritzker (eds.), *Encyclopedia of Creativity,* Vol. 1. San Diego, Calif.: Academic Press, 1999.

Jackowitz, E. R., and Watson, M. W. "Development of Object Transformation in Early Pretend Play." *Developmental Psychology,* 1980, *16,* 543–549.

Kellogg, R. *Analyzing Children's Art.* Palo Alto, Calif.: National Press Books, 1970.

Pufall, P. B., Parker, L., and Falck, J. "A Developmental Study of Children's Drawing Style." Paper presented at the meeting of the Jean Piaget Society, Philadelphia, June 1982.

Siegler, R. S. "Cognitive Variability: A Key to Understanding Cognitive Development." *Current Directions in Psychological Science,* 1994, *3,* 1–5.

Smith, N. R. "How a Picture Means." In H. Gardner and D. P. Wolf (eds.), *Early Symbolization.* New Directions for Child Development, no. 3. San Francisco: Jossey-Bass, 1979.

Somerville, S. C. "Individual Drawing Styles of Three Children from Five to Seven Years." In D. Rogers and J. A. Sloboda (eds.), *The Acquisition of Symbolic Skills.* New York: Plenum, 1983.

Van Sommers, P. "The Conservation of Children's Drawing Strategies: At What Level Does Stability Persist?" In D. Rogers and J. A. Sloboda (eds.), *The Acquisition of Symbolic Skills.* New York: Plenum, 1983.

Wieder, C. G. "Child Art and the Emergence of Learning Styles." *Visual Arts Research,* 1998, *24,* 21–27.

MALCOLM W. WATSON is *professor of psychology at Brandeis University in Waltham, Massachusetts.*

SUSAN NOZYCE SCHWARTZ is *a clinical psychologist at the Center for Preventive Psychiatry in White Plains, New York.*

Individual styles in girls' drawings over a four-year period were discernible across six-month intervals but not when the interval spanned menarche, indicating a discontinuity in style related to maturation in other developmental domains.

Continuity of Styles in the Drawings of Adolescent Girls

Deborah J. Laible, Malcolm W. Watson, Elissa Koff

Style in a painting or drawing is an abstract quality. It cannot be easily defined or expressed in words, although it is an important concept in understanding a work of art. Style is the artist's characteristic form of expression; it permeates and integrates every aspect of his or her work (Roman, 1968). Although there is no agreement on a definition (see Chapter Five), philosophers, psychologists, and artists often refer to three components of style: (1) subject matter (or content), (2) form (or technique), and (3) expression (or intended meaning) (Hartley, Somerville, Jensen, and Eliefja, 1982). Despite its importance, style has received little attention in research on art and drawing development relative to other issues, such as the general sequence of techniques and skills in children's drawing (Di Leo, 1970; Gardner, 1980; Rosenblatt and Winner, 1988; Winner, 1982), intellectual ability and its relation to art (Harris, 1963), and the influence of schooling and culture on drawing ability (Cox, 1993; Fortes, 1981; Matlew and Connolly, 1996).

Research on style that has focused on adult artists suggests that adults have a distinctive style that can often be easily discriminated by those familiar with their works (Hartley and Homa, 1981). When this distinctive style first emerges, however, is a point of dispute. Gardner (1980) suggests that an individual does not develop a distinctive style in any creative field until adolescence because style evolves out of the adolescent's struggle to discover his or her identity. Research on this issue, however, is lacking, and some studies (for example, Hartley and others, 1982) contradict Gardner's hypothesis and suggest that a distinctive style (with some stability over time) may be present in the drawings of young children.

In a study involving the artwork of three five-year-old children, for two of the three children, Hartley and others (1982) found that judges rated two matched pictures by the same artist as being significantly more similar than two matched pictures by different artists. In addition, the researchers found that judges familiar with the artwork of the three children could learn to classify (at levels above chance and from among distracter pictures) previously unseen drawings by the two children with discernible styles. Finally, judges could agree on verbal descriptions of their styles. These findings suggest that for two of the three five-year-old artists, some stylistic elements remained constant across drawings and that these elements might constitute each child's "personal" style.

Does personal style change with shifts in drawing skills or shifts in other, related developmental domains such as cognitive development? Research has shown that drawing skills become more graphically differentiated and realistic during the elementary school years, although debate exists on whether these changes in drawing skills are domain-specific or linked to general developmental progressions (see Karmiloff-Smith, 1990; Vinter 1994). Nevertheless, it has not been determined whether individual characteristics of children's drawings (for example, line quality) remain stable across these improvements in drawing abilities.

Other than the studies presented in this volume, one of the few studies that has addressed the stability of artistic style in young children provides some evidence for its stability (Somerville, 1983). Somerville collected representative drawings from the three five-year-old artists in the original study by Hartley and others (1982). New drawings were solicited from the same three artists nine and twenty-one months after the original study. Judges were trained to distinguish each of the three young artists' drawing styles until they could accurately separate the original drawings into subsets done by each artist. The judges were then tested on their ability to classify the new drawings. To ensure that judges were relying on the style of each artist to make their classifications, distracter pictures by artists of similar ages were included in the set of drawings they were judging. Despite obvious changes in the children's graphic skills, the judges were able to classify correctly many of the new drawings, even though they were produced as much as twenty-one months after the drawings with which judges were familiar. This study provides evidence that artistic style may have some consistency across time, at least across the late preschool years.

The judges in the Somerville (1983) study were not entirely accurate in reclassifying the young children's drawings, however, suggesting that some elements of style may change across age. One challenge for researchers is to determine which elements change and which remain stable. This task is complicated by the fact that development of individual artistic style is likely affected by the extent of training in art a child has had. It is also possible that artistic style may be more discernible at certain points in development than at others, as two studies in this volume suggest (see Chapters

Three and Five). For example, Watson and Schwartz, in Chapter Three, found that artistic style is more discernible in the drawings of preschoolers, kindergartners, and second graders than in the drawings of fourth graders.

The research on continuity in artistic style up to this time has been conducted on the artwork of young children or adults. To understand whether distinctive styles remain stable across all ages and to fill in the gaps in our understanding of the developmental sequence, research is needed on older children and adolescents as well. Adolescence would seem to be an especially important period in which to examine the development of artistic style because important changes in artistic ability and sensitivity to art occur during this time. For example, by the age of nine years, children begin to use perspective in their drawings, although they often fail to produce it correctly (Winner, 1982). The ability to use perspective in drawings becomes increasingly complex and accurate throughout adolescence (Gardner, 1980; Winner, 1982) and may induce a discontinuity in style.

Adolescence also brings about a shift in children's sensitivity to other qualities of art. Rosenblatt and Winner (1988) investigated the ability of children to respond to both expression and line quality in drawings. In their study, children were first shown some original pictures and then asked to complete drawings that differed only in quality of line or mood from the original drawings but to use the same style as was in the original. The researchers reasoned that if children were aware of differences in line quality and expressiveness, they would complete the drawings with similar qualities. Not before early adolescence were children successful in producing both the appropriate mood and line quality for the drawings.

By early adolescence, it seems, children demonstrate an increasing ability to understand the complex dimensions involved in a work of art and to include these complex dimensions in their own art, but it is unclear how this new understanding and ability affect a child's artistic style. Does style undergo a significant shift as a result of these changes? Is artistic style more stable and generally immune to the graphic advancements of the artist and his or her greater understanding of the qualities of art? Of course, the direction of causality could be bi-directional, further complicating the situation.

The current study examined whether a discernible style is present in the drawings of girls entering adolescence and, if so, how this style changes throughout early adolescence. Unlike previous studies on artistic style conducted mainly on preschool and early elementary school–aged children, this study involved older children (all girls) and spanned a four-year period (grades 6–9), during which important developmental changes occurred. If style can be shown to be discernible throughout the transitions of early adolescence, it would suggest that, by the time of entry into adolescence, artistic style has become a stable, distinctive characteristic that is resistant to change.

On the basis of past research (for example, Somerville, 1983), we predicted that the judges would be able to discern the style of the early adolescent girls in drawings that were produced close in time, but we also predicted that judges would be unable to discern the style of the girls in drawings that were produced far apart in time.

Because drawings were collected over four years, beginning in grade 6, most girls experienced menarche (the onset of menstruation) during this time. It was predicted that the onset of menstruation—a major life transition—could affect the stability of style, making it more difficult to match drawings that had been produced before and after menarche. Menarche provides a clear-cut life transition that is usually accompanied by social changes in role expectations and peer relationships (Koff and Rierdan, 1993; Koff, Rierdan, and Silverstone, 1978) that are independent of drawing skills. Using menarche as a marker provided us with a good assessment of whether such major developmental transitions may disrupt the continuity of artistic style. Thus, we predicted that by early adolescence artistic style would be discernible but that the major developmental transition of menarche would cause instability in style.

We also examined how other variables inherent in drawings affect the ability of judges to discriminate style in works of art. These variables included artistic ability, shading, amount of detail, use of space, line quality, and realism. A unique feature of this study was that the general theme of the drawings of each artist was limited to line drawings of female and male human figures. Even though Pufall and Pesonen (Chapter Five) persuasively argue that content is a major component of style, by holding content constant we could assess more precisely the contributions of other characteristics to the distinctiveness of style.

Most previous studies on artistic style have not examined how elements inherent in drawings affect a judge's ability to discern style. Because there are so few studies of the elements constituting artistic style, no a priori predictions were made about the relation of these elements to the distinctiveness of style. The only exception was artistic ability. We predicted that the more accomplished the artist, the more distinct her style would be.

Method, Artists, and Judges

We analyzed the artwork of twelve girls in this study, randomly selected from a larger sample of girls participating in a four-year longitudinal study focusing on psychological changes associated with pubertal development (Koff and Rierdan, 1993; Rierdan and Koff, 1990). At the start of the study, girls were in grade 6 and had a mean age of 11.5 years. The entire sample consisted of 209 white girls attending public schools in middle-class suburbs of Boston. Girls responded to an extensive questionnaire administered twice yearly, in two sessions that were one week apart, over a four-year period. At each six-month administration, girls were asked to draw a person and then to draw another person of the opposite sex. Over the four-year period, each girl drew a total of eight sets of pictures (one boy and one girl at each test administration); six of these picture sets from each girl were used in this study. The picture sets included drawings from the first, second, seventh, and eighth administrations, as well as the picture sets from the two sessions that spanned the time of each girl's menarche. To be included in this study, a girl had to achieve menarche between the third and sixth administrations (that is, between approximately 12.5 to 14.0 years of age).

Another twelve girls were randomly selected from the same sample, and their drawings served as controls. For these girls also, menarche had to occur sometime between the third and sixth administrations. The control pictures were used as distracters in the judging process described later. A total of twenty-four distracter pictures, two from each of the girls, were used in the study.

Two sets of twelve judges were used for this study. Judges were junior, senior, and postbaccalaureate studio art or art history majors and minors from a small, private liberal arts college. Eight male and sixteen female judges participated in the study. Their mean age was 21.2 years, and they had taken an average of nine studio art or art history college classes. They were therefore deemed to be appropriate judges of art because of their experience and exposure to art.

Procedure

For the first part of the study, twelve judges were shown each of the picture sets (one drawing of a male and one drawing of a female) made by the twelve girls selected to be in the target artist group. Each judge independently completed ratings of the drawings; judges could not talk to each other or see the ratings of the other judges. The judges rated each of the 72 picture sets (12 girls × 6 picture sets) for each of the following qualities: (1) *artistic ability* (How good an artist is the girl who created the drawings?), (2) *intensity of shading* (How much light and dark contrast is present in the drawings?), (3) *amount of detail* (How much detail does the artist use in the clothing, hair, and face of the people in her drawings?), (4) *amount of space filled* (How much space does the artist fill with her drawings of the people?), (5) *boldness of line* (How dark is the line used to create the person in the drawing?), and (6) *realism* (How true to life are the people in the drawings?). Each of the six qualities was rated on a 7-point Likert scale (1 = *a low score or low amount of a particular quality*, 7 = *a high score or high amount of that quality*). The judges were asked to use the entire 7 points on each scale in their picture ratings.

Judges were informed of the entire age range and number of girls and knew that the picture sets were completed by the girls over a four-year period. No more information about the girls or their drawings was given to them. Judges viewed all the drawings before they made their ratings for each of the individual sets and were asked to rate the pictures relative to all other picture sets. Reliability for the twelve judges was high for all six ratings across all drawings (Cochran's Q analysis, alpha = .87 for artistic ability, alpha = .90 for intensity of shading, alpha = .93 for amount of detail, alpha = .98 for amount of space filled, alpha = .90 for boldness of the line, and alpha = .90 for realism).

For the second part of this study, each of the seventy-two picture sets of the target artists was matched either with a picture set from a control artist (a distracter) or with another picture set done by the same artist at one of the other collection times. Each of the pictures from the twelve girls who were the target artists of the study were matched four times and mismatched four times. The matched sets of drawings (see Figures 4.1 through 4.8) were chosen so that the two sets done closest in time at the onset of the study (that is, the drawings done at Times 1 and 2 in grade 6) could be compared with the two sets done at the time of menarche (that is, those drawings collected between Times 3 and 6) and with the two done closest in time to the end of the study (that is, those drawings done at Times 7 and 8 in grade 9). These comparisons were chosen to assess the influence of age and menarche on the continuity of artistic style. A final match consisted of drawings from Time 1 with drawings from Time 8, so that the overall continuity of style across the four-year period could be assessed.

Figure 4.1. Picture Set Done by Artist A at Time 1 (Beginning of Grade 6)

CONTINUITY OF STYLES IN THE DRAWINGS OF ADOLESCENT GIRLS   71

Figure 4.2. Picture Set Done by Artist A at Time 2, Six Months Later

Figure 4.3. Picture Set Done by Artist B at Time 7

Figure 4.4. Picture Set Done by Artist B at Time 8, Six Months Later

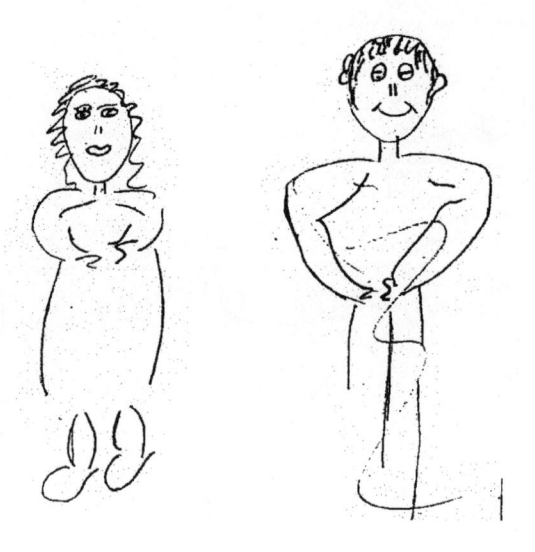

Figure 4.5. Picture Set Done by Artist C Prior to Menarche, at Time 4

CONTINUITY OF STYLES IN THE DRAWINGS OF ADOLESCENT GIRLS 73

Figure 4.6. Picture Set Done by Artist C After Menarche, at Time 5, Six Months Later

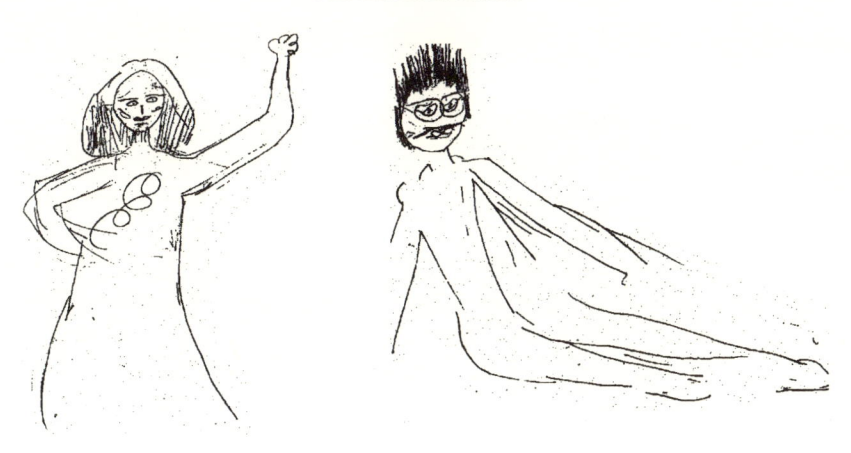

Figure 4.7. Picture Set Done by Artist D at Time 1 (Beginning of Grade 6)

74   Symbolic and Social Constraints on Children's Artistic Style

Figure 4.8. Picture Set Done by Artist D at Time 8 (End of Grade 9)

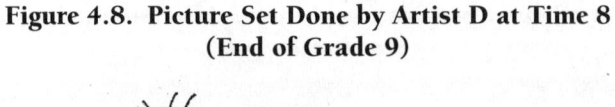

The mismatched picture sets, each consisting of one of the target artist's picture sets and one of the distracter (control) artist's picture sets, followed the same format. Thus, for example, drawings from a target artist at Time 1 were matched with drawings from a distracter artist done at Time 2. The distracter pictures were randomly matched to the pictures in the target group with the requirement that the distracter pictures appear at the same frequency as the pictures in the target group. Thus one-third of both the target and distracter pictures appear only once in the matchings; one-third appear twice; one-third appear three times.

To keep the ratings of the picture qualities from biasing assessments of the distinctiveness of drawings, a second set of twelve judges completed the following assessments. Each judge saw each of the ninety-six matched and mismatched picture sets in a random order and indicated whether each matched set was done by the same artist or by two different artists. It was made clear to judges ahead of time that, because a picture set appeared more than once, it did not mean that it was matched once with a drawing set by the same artist and once with a drawing set by another artist. As in the first part of the study, judges were informed of the number and age range of the girls involved in the study and the fact that each girl completed a number of drawings over a four-year period. Again, reliability across all picture sets for the second twelve judges was satisfactory (Cochran's Q analysis, alpha = .83).

Results

The main questions addressed in this study were whether judges could discern individual styles in the human figure drawings of early adolescent girls and, if so, whether the span of time between drawings and menarche would be related to individual styles. Another question was whether particular characteristics would be related to judges' ability to discern individual drawing styles.

Overall, judges were accurate 70.3 percent of the time in determining which of the matched and mismatched sets were done by the same and different artists. To determine whether this percentage differed significantly from chance, a two-tailed z test comparing the two proportions was used. Across all the matched and mismatched sets, $z = 3.98$, $p < .0001$, indicating that judges correctly classified the drawings at levels significantly above chance. However, judges were more accurate in identifying mismatched picture sets than matched picture sets. For the matched sets, judges' accuracy (59.7 percent) was not significantly different from chance ($z = 1.35$, $p = .17$), but for the mismatched sets, judges were accurate 80.9 percent of the time, well above chance ($z = 4.28$, $p < .0001$).

An important question was whether judges' ability to discern mismatches was based on the distinctiveness of only a few artists or on all the girls generally. To address this question, the accuracy of the judges was assessed for each target artist separately. Because the number of matched and mismatched sets for each artist was so small ($n = 8$), inferential statistics comparing these cases for each artist could not be applied. Instead the percentages of comparisons for which all judges were accurate for each artist were determined. Although the percent accuracy for each of the twelve artists was relatively high, they varied across the twelve artists from 60 to 83 percent correct. The percent correct was 65 percent or lower for four artists, indicating relatively low distinctiveness in their drawing, and it was 74 percent or higher for six artists, indicating relatively high distinctiveness in their drawing.

The primary developmental question was whether artistic style changed during the years of early adolescence. To address this question, the accuracy of judging the picture sets done across each of the four time intervals was examined. Accuracy scores, including the corresponding z-test scores and p values, can be seen in Table 4.1. Judges could attribute accurately the paired drawing sets to the same or different artist at significant, above-chance levels when the drawings by the artists were done only six months apart at Times 1 and 2 and 7 and 8 (before and after menarche). However, this accuracy of attribution was not significant at the .05 level if the drawings were done six months apart during the time that the artist's menstruation began. Thus some changes during this six-month interval disrupted the continuity of individual drawing styles. We believe it was the changes accompanying menarche. The judges did not make correct judgments about picture matches at levels significantly above chance when the pictures were done four years apart (at Times 1 and 8).

We also analyzed the relation of the drawings' qualities (that is, artistic ability, intensity of shading, amount of detail, space filled, boldness of line, and realism) to the judges' ability to discern the style of the twelve artists. To assess these relations, mean ratings of each of the six drawing qualities for each artist, obtained from the first twelve judges, were correlated with overall accuracy scores, obtained from the second twelve judges, for each artist. These correlations appear in Table 4.2.

None of the six drawing characteristics correlated significantly with accuracy scores except amount of detail, which correlated marginally ($p < .10$). Intensity of shading, amount of detail, and realism were positively correlated with judges' ratings of artistic ability. In addition, judges' ratings of intensity of shading and amount of detail were positively correlated with their ratings of realism. Finally, ratings of boldness of line were positively correlated with ratings of amount of detail.

The standard deviations of each of the six qualities were also correlated with judges' accuracy scores. These correlations were computed to determine if consistency in particular elements of style aided judges in making accurate decisions on picture sets. Once again, no significant correlations were found with accuracy scores, although the correlation between accuracy and the standard deviation for boldness of line was marginally significant ($r = -.38$, $p < .10$). Judges were less accurate with artists whose quality of line varied across picture sets. Overall, however, consistency in drawing characteristics was unrelated to judges' accuracy with paired picture sets.

Table 4.1. Comparison of Accuracy Scores of Judges Across the Four Time Intervals

Time Interval and Approximate Age	Accuracy Proportion	z Score	p Value
Premenarche, 11.5–12.0 years (Times 1 and 2)	.75	2.42	.016
At the time of menarche[a] (Times 3 and 4, 4 and 5, or 5 and 6)	.69	1.90	.057
Postmenarche, 14.5–15.0 years (Times 7 and 8)	.78	2.79	.005
Early to middle adolescence,[b] 11.5–15.0 years (Times 1–8)	.58	0.85	.400

[a]This interval cut across menarche for all girls in the study. Thus the six-month interval and age of the girls was different for each artist.

[b]This interval spanned the four years of the study; the other three time intervals spanned only six months.

Table 4.2. Correlations Between the Six Pictures' Characteristics and Judges' Accuracy

	Accuracy	Shading	Detail	Space	Realism	Boldness
Shading	.003					
Detail	.37	.55				
Space	−.16	−.01	.11			
Realism	.16	.78**	.61*	−.08		
Boldness	.21	.10	.75**	.15	.07	
Ability	.11	.77**	.85**	.12	.87**	.46

*$p < .05$; **$p < .01$.

Discussion and Conclusions

This study provides evidence that a distinctive style is present in human figure drawings done by young adolescents. Overall, judges were accurate well above chance in determining whether two paired picture sets were done by the same or different artists, but clearly some young artists demonstrated a more distinctive style than others. In making those judgments, judges were presumably attending to the consistency of some elements of style in the paired drawing sets. Because all pictures consisted of line drawings of male and female humans, variation in subject matter could not account for the distinctive styles.

Judges had much less difficulty selecting the mismatched drawing sets than the matched sets. This finding suggests that mismatched sets presented more discrepancy cues, making it easier for judges to correctly discern different artistic styles. Matched sets, in contrast, provided more ambiguous cues of differences in qualities, presumably making it more difficult for judges to determine whether the pictures were a match or not. This aspect of the picture set comparisons suggests that style is a subtle characteristic of a drawing that is difficult to recognize without clear cues of a mismatch.

It is important to note that, unlike in previous studies of artistic style (for example, Chapter Five of this volume; Somerville, 1983), judges in this study were not previously trained to select the styles of individual artists. This lack of training may have contributed to their inability to correctly identify matched sets. Despite this lack of training, however, judges could still discern individual styles. This success provides perhaps the strongest evidence that style in children's art is discernible because judges having had no experience with a given artist could nevertheless identify her style.

As predicted, judges were more accurate in making correct distinctions on paired drawing sets across narrow time spans (that is, six months apart) than when the paired sets were done four years apart. With the exception of the paired drawing set spanning each girl's menarche, judges were able to discern artistic style for both the paired drawing sets drawn within six months of each other (that is, Times 1 and 2, and Times 7 and 8), whether they were done early in adolescence or three years later.

This study provides evidence (as Watson and Schwartz do in Chapter Three) that style may be more discernible at certain times in development than others and, in fact, could be particularly affected by major developmental transitions. Judges had an easier time discerning the style in drawing sets that were done earlier or later in adolescence than in the two sets done around the time of menarche.

Menarche has been associated with changes in how the human figure is represented. Koff, Rierdan, and Silverstone (1978) found that female and male human figure drawings became more sexually differentiated after menarche; they hypothesized that these differences could be the result of the reorganization of body image as well as the reorganization of cognitive schemes. Differences in degree of sexual differentiation may account for some of the discontinuity of artistic style observed in this study. However, other cognitive changes associated with menarche could account for discontinuities. Without more research on the cognitive changes that accompany menarche, it is difficult to speculate about the cognitive changes that could affect artistic development. Clearly, though, shifts in graphic representations associated with other developmental changes are worth pursuing in research.

The fact that the judges were not accurate when evaluating drawing sets that spanned the four years of the study suggests that artistic style has not yet become highly stable in early adolescence. Clearly, over that four-year period the artists changed the way they represented human figures in form, meaning, and perhaps in other aspects of content that we did not assess. Although it is possible that a change in graphic abilities could account for these stylistic changes, most individuals' graphic skills, unless they receive formal art training, improve little from the onset to the end of adolescence (Winner, 1982). The changes in artistic ability observed in this study were likely due to more than just a change in drawing skill.

Despite the possible influences of cognitive skills and sexual differentiation, none of the qualities that we assessed correlated with the degree to which judges could discern individual styles. Similarly, contrary to prediction, the artistic ability of the artist did not predict judges' discrimination of style. Therefore the particular elements of style that judges used in making their judgments about the paired picture sets is still unknown.

Although this study did not focus specifically on which qualities of a drawing correlated with ratings of either realism or artistic ability, several qualities did predict these ratings. Pictures that were rated by the judges as realistic and high in artistic ability were also rated as being high in detail and shading.

Like the previous studies of artistic style, this study was limited in the number of child artists it was able to evaluate. Future researchers should find creative ways to add more artists without overwhelming judges with the number of pictures to be assessed. Using only six pictures from twelve artists in this study resulted in ninety-six paired picture sets; had we included more artists, we would have risked fatiguing the judges. An improved design for future research might be to use the same procedure but to recruit more sets of judges and more artists but to limit each set of judges to the evaluation of only a small number of artists.

Research about artistic style has been limited, despite the fact that an understanding of artistic style has important consequences for both art and psychology. More research is needed not only to understand developments (such as menarche) that affect artistic style but to understand the meaning of shifts in artistic style to overall development.

On an applied level, our research has implications for art education. Art educators could take into account shifts in children's art development to foster a student's individual style. On a psychological level, shifts in artistic style are undoubtedly reflective of changes in other domains of development, as was demonstrated in this study of young adolescents; thus an understanding of the continuity and discontinuity of artistic style could increase our understanding of development more generally.

References

Cox, M. V. *Children's Drawings of the Human Figure*. Mahwah, N.J.: Erlbaum, 1993.
Di Leo, J. H. *Young Children and Their Drawings*. New York: Brunner/Mazel, 1970.
Fortes, M. "Talensi Children's Drawings." In B. Lloyd and J. Gay (eds.), *Universals of Human Thought: Some African Evidence*. Cambridge, England: Cambridge University Press, 1981.
Gardner, H. *Artful Scribbles: The Significance of Children's Drawings*. New York: Basic Books, 1980.
Harris, D. *Children's Drawings as Measures of Intellectual Maturity*. Orlando, Fla.: Harcourt Brace, 1963.
Hartley, J. L., and Homa, D. "Abstraction of Stylistic Concepts." *Journal of Experimental Psychology: Human Learning and Memory*, 1981, 7, 33–46.
Hartley, J. L., Somerville, S., Jensen, D.V.C., and Eliefja, C. C. "Abstraction of Individual Style from the Drawings of Five-Year-Old Children." *Child Development*, 1982, 53, 1193–1214.
Karmiloff-Smith, A. "Constraints on Representational Change: Evidence from Children's Drawings." *Cognition*, 1990, 34, 57–83.
Koff, E., and Rierdan, J. "Advanced Pubertal Development and Eating Disturbance in Early Adolescent Girls." *Journal of Adolescent Health Care*, 1993, 14, 433–439.
Koff, E., Rierdan, J., and Silverstone, E. "Changes in Representation of Body Image as a Function of Menarcheal Status." *Developmental Psychology*, 1978, 14, 635–642.
Matlew, M., and Connolly, K. "Human Figure Drawings by Schooled and Unschooled Children in Papua New Guinea." *Child Development*, 1996, 67, 2743–2762.
Rierdan, J., and Koff, E. "Premenarcheal Predictors of the Experience of Menarche." *Journal of Adolescent Health Care*, 1990, 11, 404–407.
Roman, K. *Encyclopedia of the Written Word: A Lexicon for Graphology and Other Aspects of Writing*. New York: Ungar, 1968.
Rosenblatt, E., and Winner, E. "The Art of Children's Drawing." *Journal of Aesthetic Education*, 1988, 22, 3–15.

Somerville, S. C. "Individual Drawing Styles of Three Children from Five to Seven Years." In D. Rogers and J. A. Sloboda (eds.), *The Acquisition of Symbolic Skills*. New York: Plenum, 1983.

Vinter, A. "Hierarchy Between Graphic Production Rules in the Drawing of Elementary Figures." In C. Faure, P. Kreuss, G. Lorette, and A. Vinter (eds.), *Advances in Handwriting and Drawing: A Multidisciplinary Approach*. Paris: Europia, 1994.

Winner, E. *Invented Worlds: The Psychology of the Arts*. Cambridge, Mass.: Harvard University Press, 1982.

DEBORAH J. LAIBLE *is assistant professor of psychology at Southern Methodist University in Dallas, Texas.*

MALCOLM W. WATSON *is professor of psychology at Brandeis University in Waltham, Massachusetts.*

ELISSA KOFF *is professor of psychology at Wellesley College in Wellesley, Massachusetts.*

We develop the proposition that children's drawing style is sustained and developed in "artworlds"—a symbolic reality constrained by social valuings of art and opportunities to do art, as well as children's personal themes and representational skills that change systematically over development and with artistic experience.

Looking for the Development of Artistic Style in Children's Artworlds

Peter B. Pufall, Tuuli Pesonen

In this chapter we explore persistence and change in children's artistic style, specifically their style in graphic media. *Style* is a term with a rich set of meanings in both folk discourse and academic study. We do not offer an a priori definition of style but rather a promise to reveal a clearer conceptualization of it by situating our analysis in a social context called *artworld* (Becker, 1982; Parsons, 1988; Pufall, 1997). Artworlds are loosely structured social organizations within which people cooperate to create favorable conditions for producing works of art (Becker, 1982). These are social worlds that are mutually constructed by children and adults for the purpose of creating images or forms from a variety of media. These worlds emerge in different places and for different reasons. For example, artworlds of early childhood are realized at kitchen tables at home and easels in a classroom. Adults enter these worlds in different ways. Sometimes they merely promote them by urging children to draw, paint, or sculpt with the materials they provide but with little or no instruction about what it means to carry out those creative activities. In other cases they formally instruct children about the what and why of the adult artworld.

Children participate in these worlds at several levels, giving them form and purpose. They explore the media and the various marks that different materials make as they are brushed or dragged across a surface. As children gain control over the media, they begin to explore personal

---

We are indebted to Lelá Gandini for the scholarly contributions she made to the development of our studies of style, to Rebecca Whitin, Pamela Maryanski, and Ellen Kitchell, who assisted with this research, and to the Office of Admissions at Smith College, who supported their work through the STRIDE Program.

themes and narratives within the images they create. In this chapter we concentrate on how children's functioning in their artworlds affects the development of their individual style.

By situating style in this context, we have tried to avoid two extremes. One is to conceive of style as exclusively a formal property of art that has meaning without making any reference to what the artist did or intended to create. At the other extreme is the assumption that style is embodied fully in the content of an artist's work. Cohen-Shalev (1993) describes this as the *core dilemma* of the artist's work. For us artistic style is psychologically meaningful (and we presume historically as well) only when our conceptualization of style embodies both *how* and *what* we draw.

The chapter is divided into two sections. The first is a brief historical perspective on artistic style that is intended to help us understand the intellectual struggle to conceptualize style. From this analysis we offer some insights into the nature of style in children's art.

The second section summarizes evidence for persistence and change in children's artistic style prospectively and retrospectively. The prospective analysis explores the perceived persistence of a child's style at a younger age over a three-year period. The retrospective analysis explores whether the style we perceive in children's art at a later age allows us to see their earlier style. This section ends with a study relating the findings of the prospective and retrospective analyses to the stability and variation of themes children prefer to explore within their artworlds over development.

Mapping Style in Art History onto Style in Children's Art

Gombrich (1978) persuasively argues that new or former styles or periods of art were identified as deviant from *the* ideal or classical style. Fundamental to categorizing the works of a period or region in terms of style was a tendency to conflate *norm*, a social construction, with *form*, an analytical reconstruction. This led art historians to treat a revered norm as expressing an ideal or classical form. All art was evaluated with respect to this classical form, achieving a renaissance or reflecting an unfortunate deviation from the human quest to touch perfection through art.

This is not to suggest that all historians have failed to recognize the historical myopia and cultural chauvinism implicit in appeals to an ideal or classical style. Some have offered analytical stances intended to be culturally neutral. Gombrich (1978) offers Wölfflin's model of style as an example. His approach is presumed to be neutral insofar as it entails a set of analytical dimensions within which any piece of work can be described, and therefore the style of a period, group, or individual could be discovered if there were a consistent pattern of description across several creations. He identifies five dichotomized dimensions: linearity versus painterly, plane versus depth, closed versus open form, multiplicity versus unity, and clarity versus obscurity. If we assume that these dimensions exhaust the formal properties of artistic creations, they serve as analytical tools for describing and comparing works of art without passing judgment that one is better or worse, more or less developed, or closer or farther from perfectibility.

This method fails to consider *how* or *why* art is done, nor does it speak to the question of whether the art is beautiful or why people of other cultures and during other historical times painted what they did and as they did. As we move through a gallery, we could adopt a formal stance exclusively, but it would be unsatisfying to do so; we experience more than a work's formal structure. We wonder why the artist painted what she did and what she intended to share with or reveal to us. We delight in purchasing art so that we can appreciate its beauty as part of our everyday life. We feel at one with the artist when we believe we are directly perceiving the artist's *intention* (Bloom, 1996).

Adding aesthetics and intentionality to the mix of experiences by which to categorize works of art undermines the presumed objectivity of the *neutralist's* stance. An example of the problematic position of the neutralist can be drawn from the debate over change in the aesthetic quality of children's painting and drawing from four to ten years of age. Developmental scientists and educators identified with Harvard's Project Zero used Goodman's analytical properties of aesthetics (for example, expressiveness and repleteness), which are like Wölfflin's more global properties identified earlier. Presumably they describe the aesthetic content of art without allusion to meaning. Empirical studies from this project suggest a curvilinear pattern of aesthetic development (Carothers and Gardner, 1979; Davis, 1997; Winner, 1982). The paintings of four- and five-year-old children were aesthetically rich, by Goodman's standard, whereas those of the children in early- to mid-grade school did not embody these aesthetic characteristics to the same extent. The fact that their studies revealed that some adolescents and adults once again expressed Goodmanian aesthetics to the same extent as preschool-age children gave rise to the conclusion that, at least in Western societies, aesthetic development follows a curvilinear path. This is *a* path but not *the* path for all, as many continue to draw and paint in an aesthetic style that emphasizes a detailed and rigid realism (Davis, 1997).

Although the empirical validity of a curvilinear developmental path of Goodmanian aesthetics has been accepted, some have challenged the proposition that Goodman's aesthetics are neutral (Duncum, 1986; Wilson, 1997). They point to the cultural bias of his categories. In their view his aesthetics reflect the values of only some aspects of Western art and may or may not reflect the aesthetics of non-Western cultures. Even with respect to Western cultures, Goodman's system fails to value the continuous development of children's capacity to create more and more representational artwork. The cultural embeddedness of Goodman's aesthetic categories is revealed as well in the sample of judges who are likely to detect these qualities in children's art. Artists, historians, or art dealers who are deeply involved in Western artistic traditions are more likely to see these qualities in art; those less trained in this tradition are more likely to fail to see them. Indeed, young children themselves—the producers of art marked by Goodmanian aesthetics—do not appear to value it. Instead they appear to value their art and the art of others against a standard of realism. Four- and five-year-old children reject their own work when it is expressive and replete but not representative, and they favor the more precise representations created by children two or three years older than they are (Goodnow, Wilkins, and Dawes, 1986).

Young children clearly fail to understand the inherent attractiveness of their own work and give no indication that they see it as "better" or "prettier" than the work of older children. It could be argued that the ambiguity of these terms is due to the fact that "better" (and "prettier" to a lesser extent) depends on sufficient social experiences from which children can extract the criteria by which cultures partition artistic domains. However, the reliability of children's replies suggests that they are co-constructive agents in the process of developing their aesthetics. There is considerable consensus in the research literature, which is based on studies of children reared in Western cultures, that young children value drawings that *depict* objects or persons realistically over those that *convey* the artist's reactions to those objects symbolically or abstractly (for example, Milbrath, 1995, 1998).

Ultimately, however, we would be missing the point if we were to focus only on the methodological uncertainties involved when children and adults are asked to evaluate the same object or event. It is epistemologically contradictory to expect that children *interpret* the question in exactly the same way adults do yet offer contradictory *answers*. The central criticism of Wilson (1997), among others, is the improbability of identifying a neutral aesthetics that does not emerge from a cultural heritage and is not involved in the process of both conveying and maintaining meaning within the community that gave it life.

Just as in aesthetics, our understanding of style involves resolving a tension between a neutralist's and culturalist's position. The interdependency of the meaning of an art work and the style in which it is done is at the heart of Rothschild's claim that style "summarizes much that is deeply significant about a person or a society" (1960, p. 171). This claim is not conceptually satisfying, as it leaves too much to our imagination about how we could characterize stylistic summaries of core values and experiences. Although sympathetic with Rothchild's claim, Mendolowitz (1963) moves us closer to a psychological theory of style in his book, *Children Are Artists*. For him the artistic process can be partitioned into *what* children draw, paint, or sculpt, that is, the subject matter or content they intend to express or depict, versus *how* children draw, that is, their style. The child's artistic creations cannot be equated with their objective content such as a mother, father, or self but must be understood in terms of the child's subjective experiences of pleasure, excitement, and at times pain associated with the objective content. Children draw what they do to relive, control, and understand their experiences, not just to get the images right. Just as we cannot fully understand what children draw within a superficial description of the content of their art, according to Mendolowitz, style cannot be reduced to techniques for controlling media. How children draw is constrained by the child's personal experiences, personality, and physical competencies.

Gardner's notion of style (1980) is consistent with Mendolowitz's broad definition of *personal style* (1963). His stylistic categories of *patterners* and *dramatists* are rooted in aspects of self that affect not only how children draw but also how they play, problem solve, and create peer relationships. At the level of the individual, this understanding of style is broadly akin to personality and self-esteem, which are presumed to mediate a wide variety of adaptive, everyday activities. More narrowly, when so construed artistic style is akin to learning styles such as impulsivity versus reflectivity.

There is obvious danger in identifying parallels between historical and psychological development. In fact, that is not our purpose in the mapping we have created. Our purpose is to use art history to draw out some issues that are fundamental to any study of artistic style and, in this case, persistence and change in style. Whether we focus on styles of a historical period or within an individual, we have to grapple with what we mean by style. We have to decide whether we will take a *neutralist's* stance, which presumes that style can be understood, independent of a cultural-historical context, or a *culturalist's* stance, which presumes that styles are inherent in cultures and neglect the individual's imprint.

Artworlds and Persistence and Change in the Style of Children

From studies of gifted children, artistic skill appears to be the cornerstone for constructing artworlds (Golomb, 1995; Winner, 1996). Gifted children demonstrate skillfulness very early in development, and they quickly exploit their repertoire of skills to produce large volumes of art that explore a limited number of themes. Their artworlds appear to be more than sources of pleasure; they have purpose. Within them, children reflect on themes and the means by which themes and artistry are interrelated. We believe that this personal exploration of *theme* individualizes artworlds.

Here we explore the proposition that to look at children's art is to enter their artworlds. When we perceive a new piece of art as Suzy's or in the manner of Suzy's art, we do so based on the factors that constrained her world as she drew or painted: the themes she explores, the conceptual issues these explorations raise, and the artistic devices she uses to symbolize those issues. It is our hypothesis that the artistic process of each child is distinctive because of the way each one works out the relation between depicting and conveying what he or she intends to communicate (Mendelowitz, 1963).

Are the artworlds of "ordinary" children different from those of the gifted? Are they dominated by special themes expressed in discriminable styles? If children have individual styles discriminable within at least brief periods of life, for example, a few months to a year, does style persist or does it change over time? In the remainder of this chapter, we offer tentative answers to these questions based on three studies we have carried out together. The first two studies are paradigmatically similar, drawing on a discrimination paradigm introduced by Hartley and others (Hartley, Somerville, Von Cziesch Jensen, and Eliefja, 1982; Somerville, 1983). At the core of this discrimination paradigm is the question of whether or not adults can perceive a distinctiveness in children's drawings or paintings; that is, can adults perceive children's art as categorically distinctive?

At one level of analysis we are trying to determine whether or not there is a formal, invariant structure in the works of children that transcends the specifics of their creations. At another level, we are assuming that individual style entails both what children draw and how they draw, and that adults discern *both* of these properties when they distinguish the individual categories of children's art. Although the first two studies have a similar conceptual goal, that is, to assess questions about the persistence of artistic style over development, they differ in one fundamental way. In the first study we address this question prospectively. If we extract the style of young children's art from a body of their work, will that knowledge allow us to differentiate their later artwork from the art of other children? In short, is there a commonality in their younger and older work that transcends the development of artistic skills and changes in their preferred artistic themes?

The second study addresses the question retrospectively. If we extract the style of older children from a body of their art, will this knowledge allow us to differentiate their earlier work from the work of other children?

Study 1: A Prospective Analysis of Children's Style

Tuuli Pesonen was the principal investigator of the prospective analysis of artistic style (Pesonen and Pufall, 1997). *Prospective analysis* means looking for the persistence of style over age. Methodologically it entails judges trying to extract a child's artistic style at a younger age, say from a body of work done at age five years, and then determining whether or not those judges can recognize the work this child did at subsequent ages, based on knowledge of the child's style.

We examined the issue of the existence and persistence of artistic style in a representative sample of paintings and drawings by three children (Ant, Bat, and Cat) from age five to nine years. Their artwork was sampled from an archive of children's works systematically maintained by the school they attended. Broadly speaking, their art had two purposes. On the one hand, much of the work was done at the children's leisure for their own amusement. On the other hand, because the school embraced an educational-developmental philosophy that valued drawing, painting, and sculpting as symbolic activities by which children could represent questions and understandings, a substantial portion of their art was done as an integral part of traditional educational activities such as history, literature, social, and natural science. Each year, each child's graphic and plastic art, as well as the prose and poetry collected in the child's portfolio, was the basis for teachers' evaluations of the children's educational progress and overall development.

There is a conceptual advantage to working with this type of data set when studying artistic style. On the upside, this art is more likely to express artistic individuality in the sense discussed by Mendolowitz (1963), Rothschild (1960), and Gardner (1980). And because their work comes from an artworld over which children have considerable control, we can assume they were engaged in making images that went beyond depicting objects or scenes to conveying the children's understanding and feeling. In this sense, working with this type of art seems to offer a more valid test of the questions related to the existence and persistence of artistic style.

Persistence of style was studied using a perceptual learning technique (Hartley and others, 1982). Judges were asked to categorize samples of the artwork as the works of Ant, Bat, or Cat. Given the freedom children appeared to have in creating their art, there is a methodological challenge in creating matched sets of artwork. To the best extent possible the drawings were matched for content, the use of color media versus pencil, size of the drawings, and size of the paper on which the drawings were done. This meant we had samples of art that were consistent across children on these variables; however, it also meant that within groups of children we had sets of art that varied along each of these dimensions. We hypothesized that judges who successfully categorize the art do so based on perceptual information that is both common to the art of each child and at the same time differentiates one child's work from another.

There were several phases to the study. In the first phase, or learning phase, adult judges with no special training in the arts or child development were shown twenty-seven slides of the children's art done when they were approximately five years old. Within this set, each child produced nine pieces. As each slide was projected, the judges identified which of the three children they thought had done it. Judges were told whether they were right or wrong; if they were wrong, they were not told which child had actually done the work. Judges were shown the sets over and over again until they reached a predetermined criterion.

Once the judges reached criterion for each child's art, they participated in three generalization phases. In each phase, judges were shown eighteen slides, six of art done by each child. Of those six slides, three had not been shown to the judges during the learning phase ("new" art), and three had been shown during learning ("old" art). In the first generalization phase the new art was sampled from work done when children were five years old, that is, at the age when they did the drawings shown in the learning phase. In the second phase the new paintings were sampled from art done when the children were six years old; in the third phase, the art was sampled from that done when the children were eight years old. In each generalization phase the "old" art was done when the children were five years of age and had been seen during the learning phase. A different set of three "old" pieces was shown in each generalization phase.

In contrast to the learning phase, in each generalization phase the sets of eighteen slides were shown only once. Correct categorization that is significantly above chance ($p = .33$, or a one in three chance of being correct when guessing whether it is a work of Ant, Bat, or Cat) is evidence that the style extracted from the learning phase was used by the judges to differentiate the "new" art as Ant's, Bat's, or Cat's. Obviously, successful categorizing during generalization is a more stringent test that judges have extracted an abstract style during the learning phase rather than succeeding by memorizing the drawings of each child.

Adult judges accurately categorized the art of each child in three or four trials, that is, after having seen the entire learning set of twenty-four slides three or four times. They also reliably identified which children painted the "new" art in all three generalization phases (see Figure 5.1). These findings establish that the judges detected the distinctive styles of each child during the learning phase and used that knowledge to attribute correctly much of the new art to these children. As Hartley and others (1982) did, we found that judges were less and less accurate over phases of generalization; however, in contrast to their findings, judges in our study continued to differentiate the later work of children significantly above a chance level.

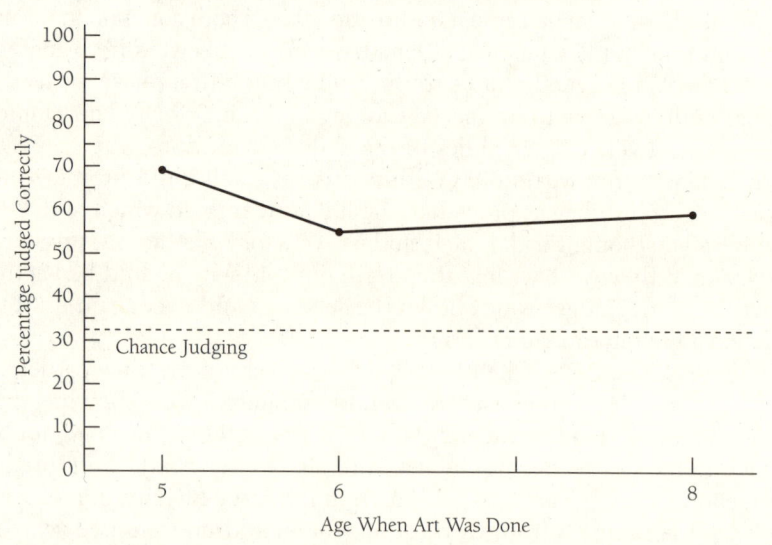

Figure 5.1. Study 1: Prospective Analysis

Age When Art Was Done

Note: Shown is the generalization function when learning artistic style is based on art done by children at age five years. The function is expressed in terms of the percentage of children's "new" art judged correctly at three different ages.

This extended persistence of style may be due to the fact that this art emerged from the interests and goals of each child's artworld. Even when their drawings were intended to represent their issues being covered in specific subject matter, they had freedom to include what they thought to be central, and they were given some latitude in how they would represent that knowledge in their artworlds. By contrast, Hartley and others (1982) generated their database by giving children a limited set of options to exercise in a testing situation. In short, the success of our judges at differentiating children's art is linked to the fact that it represents personal issues or interests that we would expect to persist over development (we return to this hypothesis in the third study).

This is not to argue that children's artworlds do not change. They may change, even if their interests remain relatively constant. They may alter their symbolic style in order to convey those interests more effectively (Lindstrom, 1957). Or they may change when children begin to explore new interests or issues in their artworlds. These new issues undoubtedly bring with them both conceptual and artistic problems to be solved and, as a consequence, promote change in a child's artworld. For some children this means shifting to other symbolic systems; for others it means searching out new resources in the same symbolic domain. In the latter case, we would expect stylistic change.

Examining the variation of individuals' generalization functions (see Figure 5.2) with respect to the normative development depicted in the group generalization function (see Figure 5.1) is a first step toward understanding

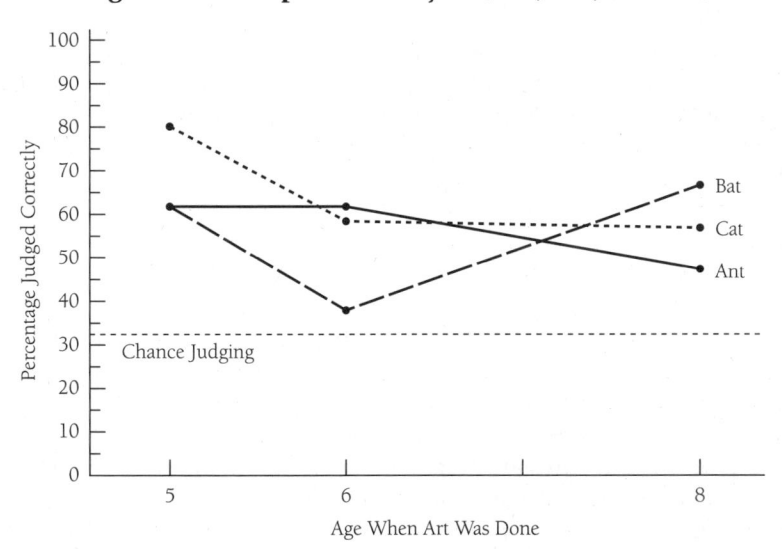

Figure 5.2. Prospective Analysis (Ant, Bat, and Cat)

Note: Shown are generalization functions when learning artistic style is based on art done by children at age five. The functions are expressed in terms of the percentage of children's "new" art that is judged correctly for each child at three different ages.

how personal interest may affect artistic style. The individual generalization functions indicate that Ant's and Cat's functions map approximately the group function, that is, although judges perceive a persistence of style in these children's art, that persistence wanes over development. Bat's function is markedly different from the norm. In his case judges reliably discriminated his work from age five and eight years but not when categorizing the work he did at age six. As we argue in the section on the relation between themes and style, differences in generalization functions appear to be related to kinds and variety of themes children develop in their artworlds.

Study 2: A Retrospective Analysis of Children's Style

Our second study of the persistence of style was a retrospective analysis (Pesonen and Pufall, 1997). From the prospective analysis it was clear that some aspect of early style of the three children in our study persisted over time. Finding evidence that style persists over development, however, does not provide an insight into what information persists or how an earlier style is integrated into a subsequent style. What we see as similar between the earlier and later art may be only a fragment or remnant of the earlier style. In fact, seeing a similarity between old and new art does not mean that we see the similarity between the earlier and later style. As we know from the learning phase, detecting style takes multiple experiences with a body of art, and that kind of experience was not provided in the generalization phases of the prospective study. These facts raise the question of whether or not judges who learn children's style based on a later body of their work will allow them to differentiate earlier works they have never seen.

To address this question we employed a retrospective method of analysis, that is, we looked for similarities in a child's art over age. Specifically, if judges understand the style of work done when a child was eight years old, will that knowledge allow them to accurately differentiate work the child did when younger? The findings that are key to the question of how the style of an earlier period is integrated into a later period comes from comparing the prospective and retrospective generalization functions. If the remnants of style children bring forward over development continue to be defining features of their later style, then the generalization functions should be symmetrical. However, if these remnants are either incidental to their more mature style or if they are integrated into a more complex style so that they are not perceived as distinctive features, then the judges should be "blind" to these features and should not see a commonality between old and new art. In that case the generalization functions should be asymmetrical.

In most respects, the manner in which the retrospective study was carried out was identical to the way we ran the prospective study. The critical difference was that in the retrospective analysis judges learned each child's artistic style on the basis of work children did during the mid-grade school years, and generalization of the extracted style was tested by having judges differentiate "new" art the children produced when they were younger.

Once again we worked with the archival art of Ant, Bat, and Cat. We did not have a large enough sample of art when the children were eight years old to create a learning set of twenty-seven pieces that controlled for content, types of medium, and so forth. Hence the learning sets came from the works children drew when they were seven years old. The three generalization phases mirrored those from Study 1. The first phase included work the children drew at age seven, the second from their work at age six, and the third from their work at age five. The generalization sets were the same size as they had been in the prospective study with the same distribution of "new" and "old" art in each set.

Judges were able to differentiate the art done when children were seven years old; however, in contrast to the prospective study it took them significantly more exposures (trials) to the learning set to reach criterion. They did generalize these styles to the children's earlier art, though once again with less and less reliability the more developmentally distant the new art was from the art of the learning set (compare Figures 5.1 and 5.3). More critical to the focus of this study, these two group generalization functions are asymmetrical. They differ significantly in their slopes, with the slope of the retrospective function steeper than that of the prospective function.

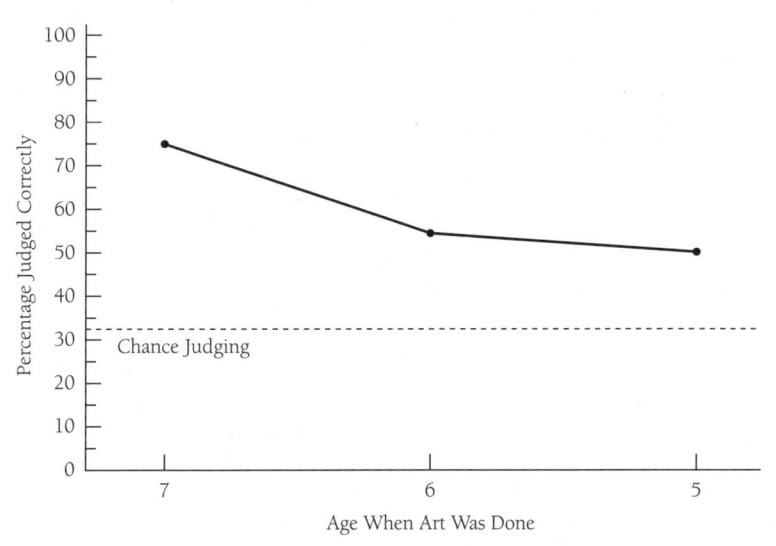

Figure 5.3. Study 2: Retrospective Analysis

Note: Shown is the generalization function when learning artistic style is based on children's art done at age seven years. The function is expressed in terms of the percentage of children's "new" art judged correctly at three different ages.

Two facts emerge from these findings. The first is that style appears to become more difficult to discern with increasing age. Given the age range represented in our work, the difference in stylistic salience may be correlated to artistic development. Earlier art is simpler. Five-year-old children do not vary the marks they use to create images to the same extent that older children do. With fewer variations to compare, it may be easier to extract the style of a younger child. Whether this analysis would continue to be true over a developmental period beyond the one we sampled can only be determined empirically. Given the differences in children's experience with art beyond age eight and the significant drop in interest in doing graphic art among many children, we would anticipate that some children would craft a distinctive style, whereas others would be more eclectic. It should be easier to discern the style of the former than the latter.

The second fact is the asymmetry of generalizations from Studies 1 and 2. Style of an earlier period is more predictive of a later period than the reverse. This suggests that what is carried forward from their earlier style can be detected in their later art if we are biased to see it. However, if we are trying to discern their later style without bias, the information common over development either becomes incidental to later style or it is integrated with a style to the extent that it cannot be seen as a specific feature of style.

There are, of course, variations on the developmental story created from grouping the children in the retrospective analysis (Figure 5.4). Ant's

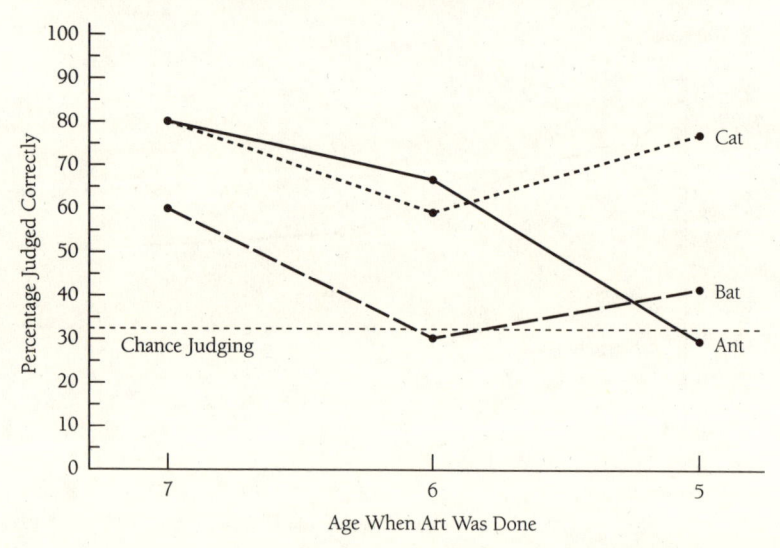

Figure 5.4. Retrospective Analysis (Ant, Bat, and Cat)

Note: Shown are generalization functions when learning artistic style is based on art done by children at age seven. The functions are expressed in terms of the percentage of children's "new" art that is judged correctly for each child at three different ages.

and Bat's generalization functions are similar to the group function; Cat's is at odds with it. As a consequence the functions of the former two children are asymmetrical with their comparable prospective functions (Figure 5.2). The slopes of the retrospective generalizations are significantly steeper than those calculated for the prospective analysis. In fact, the retrospective generalizations do not differ from chance during the third phase for either child. By contrast, Cat's pro- and retrospective generalization functions are symmetrical. In both cases there is a high level of generalization that is significantly above chance in each phase.

From the comparisons of the individual children's generalization functions, it would appear that children not only have demonstrably different artistic styles but that they appear to transform their individual styles in different ways. Children like Cat *refine* their styles but do not fundamentally change them. Children like Ant and Bat *restructure* their style so that it is fundamentally transformed over age.

Study 3: Seeking Evidence for a Dynamic Relation of Theme and Style in Children's Artworlds

We have suggested that style and theme are dynamically related in children's artworlds. More precisely, we have assumed that variations in artistic themes will lead to transformations in children's styles for conveying these themes. Because Ant, Bat, and Cat produced substantial portfolios of art at school alone, each drawing or painting over five hundred pieces over the five years covered in this study, we had a database by which we could test this hypothesis. The first step in this study was to determine whether, as gifted children (Milbrath, 1995; Winner, 1996), they showed preferences for particular themes and, if they did, whether these preferences varied over development.

In this study, *theme* is conceptualized around whether or not a drawing communicates action or animacy. This is a general level of analysis that does not take into account the range of specific life issues such as the joy of flying a kite or aggression in fights and battles. Analysis at that level would be legitimate. However, we elected to use the more general meaning of *theme* because each of the thematic categories poses distinctively different artistic problems.

We identified three thematic categories: *animate, events,* and *inanimate* (Whitin, Pesonen, and Pufall, 1998). *Animate* drawings included people and creatures, real or imagined, that were individually engaged in action such as running. This type of drawing did not convey a purpose for the action, that is, there was no way of knowing from the painting whether the person was running away from or toward something. Work was classified as depicting *event* if the purpose for the action was captured in the painting. *Inanimate* drawings included abstract work like a design or a drawing of persons or animals with no indication of action and no specification of an event in which they were participating.

Judges classified each child's art in the child's full portfolio, that is, they classified all the child's art from age five though age nine. The percentages of art within each thematic category were calculated over five one-year intervals for each child. If a child showed no bias toward one theme over another, about 33 percent of the child's drawings should have been classified into each thematic category. Using a minimum of 50 percent of classifications into thematic categories as an index of a thematic preference, we observed that all three children had distinct preferences. Taken together, the three children demonstrated a thematic preference in thirteen of the fifteen yearly intervals (five for each child).

Cat and Ant were relatively stable over five years with respect to which theme they preferred. Cat consistently drew more inanimate themes; in fact, during some years she did so almost to the neglect of the other two. Ant preferred the animate theme, but he explored the other two as well, especially during the middle years when he was six and seven years old. In contrast, Bat's preferences shifted over time. More than half of his works reflected animacy at age five, as well as at ages eight and nine years. During the middle years his preference shifted to events; like Ant though, during this era he remained interested in the other two themes as well. Hence Ant and Bat were similar insofar as they explored all three themes *within* yearly intervals and different insofar as Bat, but not Ant, had more than one thematic preference during the early grade school years.

Thematic preference and variation are systematically related to children's artistic style and especially to the perceived persistence of that style over development. Cat's style was perceived as persistent whether analyzed prospectively or retrospectively. Correlatively she painted and drew pictures that were predominately inanimate. Her work was marked by vibrant colors whether she drew abstract patterns that resembled stained glass windows, frozen scenes of princesses and princes aligned across the bottom of the page, or stylized flowers in a single row. In her portfolio, text often accompanied her drawings. This text often captured the animacy and event structure missing from her art. Her commitment to the word appears to have relieved her artworld of the artistic challenges of capturing which events take place and representing the biomechanics of action. As a consequence there is little exploration of the third dimension in her picture planes; in fact, Cat rarely composed her drawings so that they covered the entire picture plane. This is not to suggest that there was no development of artistry. Over the years her works became more vibrant in color as well as more complex and precise, even though the figures she drew were predominantly schematic.

Drawing in several themes appears to have different consequences for the development of style. The prospective and retrospective generalization functions for Ant's drawings are not symmetrical. His continued preference for animate themes may well account for the fact that adults could see prospectively a commonality in his artwork. However, his exploration of all three themes may account for the fact that the same degree of commonality was not observed in retrospective analyses. Thematic variations bring a range of conceptual and artistic problems to be solved.

Finding artistic solutions during the mid-years may have been the engine that drove the kinds of transformations in Ant's style that are best described as a restructuring rather than a refinement of his earlier style. Indeed, Ant rarely included color in his art, using pencil primarily to portray details of objects and to draw legs and arms bent to convey biomechanical action. His interest in events seems to have compelled him to create atmosphere (landscapes and airscapes) that is distributed over the entire page. The artistic repertoire needed to create the illusion that objects are at different distances in the picture plane, as well as the impression of the volume of these objects, is structurally different from skills that portray them in a flat picture plane.

Bat's developmental story appears to be a variation on Ant's. Bat's retrospective generalization function is, like Ant's, asymmetrical to his prospective function. The failure of judges to perceive any persistence in style from his later to his earlier work suggests a qualitative change in style over development. But there is more to be learned about the relation between theme and style from Bat. In contrast to both Ant and Cat, judges did not see commonality throughout Bat's development when we used a prospective analysis. Rather, they failed to perceived a commonality between his early art and his art done one year later when he had changed his thematic preferences from events to animacy, respectively. And then they were able to identify his work when he was eight years old when he had returned to the theme of his youth—events. It appears that shifts in thematic preference not only affect the emerging style but that a dramatic thematic change yields stylistic alterations that do not preserve any perceived commonality. Given the fact that Bat's retrospective generalization function represents *no persistence* over time, it would appear that the similarity seen between work at age five and eight years is due to the commonality in thematic content and not a style by which that content was conveyed.

Although variation in theme appears to be significantly related to persistence and change in artistic style, it does not appear to be related to these children's ability to communicate themes. Judges had no more difficulty identifying the themes in Ant's and Bat's art during the middle years than in the work they produced at age five or nine years. That is, even though Bat shifted his thematic preference during the middle years and Ant explored all three themes in a more balanced way at these times, judges maintained a high degree of agreement about the themes in their art. Hence it may be that choosing to vary the thematic purpose of one's art has the potential to alter the manner in which the theme is conveyed; at the same time it may not affect the clarity with which these themes are depicted.

Conclusions

Our basic intention in studying persistence and change in children's artistic style was to offer a conceptualization in the context of the construct of artworld (Becker, 1982; Parsons, 1988; Pufall, 1997). By doing so we tried to avoid conceiving of style as exclusively a formal property of art, although it is, in part. We also tried to avoid the other of extreme of identifying style with the content of art, that is, identifying the themes or motifs of children's portfolios. Again, style is partly thematic as well. But we have reasoned that children cultivate artistic style in terms of both *how* and *what* they construct in their artworlds.

By comparing the prospective and retrospective analyses of generalization functions, we have demonstrated that although detecting a child's style of an earlier age provides an insight into her art at a later age, this insight should not be equated with the fully developed style of that later age. That possibility may never exist in a strict sense and may only be approximated when there is a dominant thematic preference and little thematic variation in a child's artworld over development. We have suggested that Cat's artistic history approximates these conditions; as a consequence, the change in style over time is best described as *refinement*. By contrast, style is *restructured* when children explore a variety of themes in their artworlds, as was the case for Ant and Bat. Finally, we suggest that style and skillfulness may be psychologically independent in the sense that even when children's style is being restructured, children are remarkably skillful at communicating their artistic themes.

As we noted in our introduction to the idea of artworld, it is mutually constructed by the child and others. Artworlds are always situated in cultural contexts. As educational institutions incorporate discipline-based art education into their curricula, they should consider that the educational standards or benchmarks of these curricula are likely to be realized in different ways by children because they bring very different artworlds into the classroom. Some may have artworlds that are less bounded and in which they explore a variety of themes by a rich artistic repertoire. Others' artworlds may be narrower in both thematic diversity and artistic richness. Also we suspect that children perceive their artworlds as having very different functions. In Cat's case, her graphic art complemented her oral or written storytelling. By contrast, when Ant and Ben shared a story, they did so in the picture plane, with little if any elaboration through the spoken or written word. To encourage artistic development, we need to thoughtfully enter their artworlds, mindful that these worlds are not simply populated by artistic skills but with skills that are intended to convey meaning.

References

Becker, H. S. *Art Worlds*. Berkeley: University of California Press, 1982.
Bloom, P. "Intention, History, and Artifact Concepts." *Cognition,* 1996, *60,* 1–29.
Carothers, T., and Gardner, H. "When Children's Drawings Become Art: The Emergence of Aesthetic Production and Perception." *Developmental Psychology,* 1979, *15,* 570–580.

Cohen-Shalev, A. "The Development of Artistic Style: Transformations of a Creator's Core Dilemma." *Human Development*, 1993, *36*, 16–116.

Davis, J. "The *What* and the *Whether* of the U: Cultural Implications of Understanding Development of Graphic Symbolization." *Human Development*, 1997, *40*, 145–154.

Duncum, P. "Breaking Down the Alleged 'U' Curve of Artistic Development." *Visual Arts Research*, 1986, *12*, 43–54.

Gardner, H. *Artful Scribbles: The Significance of Children's Drawings.* New York: Basic Books, 1980.

Golomb, C. (ed.). *The Development of Artistically Gifted Children: Selected Case Studies.* Mahwah, N.J.: Erlbaum, 1995.

Gombrich, E. H. *Norm and Form: Studies in the Art of the Renaissance.* New York: Phaidon Press, 1978.

Goodnow, J. J., Wilkins, P., and Dawes, L. "Acquiring Cultural Forms: Cognitive Aspects of Socialization Illustrated by Children's Drawings and Judgments of Drawings." *International Journal of Behavioral Development*, 1986, *9*, 485–505.

Hartley, J. L., Somerville, S. C., Von Cziesch Jensen, D., and Eliefja, C. C. "Abstraction of Individual Styles from the Drawings of Five-Year-Old Children." *Child Development*, 1982, *53*, 1193–1214.

Lindstrom, M. *Children's Art: A Study of Normal Development in Children's Modes of Visualization.* Berkeley: University of California Press, 1957.

Mendolowitz, D. M. *Children Are Artists.* (2nd ed.) Stanford, Calif.: Stanford University Press, 1963.

Milbrath, C. "Germinal Motifs in the Work of a Gifted Child Artist." In C. Golomb (ed.), *The Development of Artistically Gifted Children: Selected Case Studies.* Mahwah, N.J.: Erlbaum, 1995.

Milbrath, C. *Patterns of Artistic Development in Children: Comparative Studies of Talent.* Cambridge, England: Cambridge University Press, 1998.

Parsons, M. J. "Assumptions About Art and Artworld: A Response to Critics." *Journal of Aesthetic Education*, 1988, *22*, 107–116.

Pesonen, T., and Pufall, P. B. "Searching for the Existence, Persistence, and Transformation of Style in Children's Drawing: Longitudinal Studies in Prospective and Retrospective." Poster presentation at the meeting of the Ecological Society, Amherst, Massachusetts, Apr. 1997.

Pufall, P. B. "Framing a Developmental Psychology of Art." *Human Development*, 1997, *40*, 169–180.

Rothschild, L. *Style in Art: The Dynamics of Art as Cultural Expression.* New York: Yoseloff, 1960.

Somerville, S. C. "Individual Drawing Styles of Three Children from Five to Seven Years." In D. Rogers and J. A. Sloboda (eds.), *The Acquisition of Symbolic Skills.* New York: Plenum, 1983.

Whitin, R., Pesonen, T., and Pufall, P. B. "Persisting and Changing Themes in *What* Children Draw: Implication for the *How* of Development." Poster presented at the Twenty-Eighth Annual Symposium of the Jean Piaget Society, Chicago, June 1998.

Wilson, B. "Types of Child Art and Alternative Developmental Accounts: Interpreting the Interpreters." *Human Development*, 1997, *40*, 155–168.

Winner, E. *Invented Worlds: The Psychology of the Arts.* Cambridge, Mass.: Harvard University Press, 1982.

Winner, E. *Gifted Children: Myths and Realities.* New York: Basic Books, 1996.

PETER B. PUFALL *is professor of psychology at Smith College in Northampton, Massachusetts.*

TUULI PESONEN *is youth development adviser at MY TURN, Inc., in Brockton, Massachusetts.*

Index

Adolescence, 67. See also Drawing, by girls in adolescence (case study)
Adult: as art collaborator, 6; dialogue between child and, 6–7
Albertini, G., 31, 35
Amabile, T. M., 51–52, 60, 62
Animate drawings, 93
Arnheim, R., 6, 10, 27
Art, children's. See Drawing, by girls in adolescence; Drawing, children's
Art History, 82–85
Artworld, children's: definition of, 7–8, 81; development of artistic style in, 81–96; dynamic relation of theme and style in, 93–95; and mapping style in Art History onto style in children's art, 82–85; and persistence and change in style of children, 85–86; and prospective analysis of children's style, 86–90; and retrospective analysis of children's style, 90–93
Azmitia, M., 34, 45, 46

Barrett, M. D., 15, 27
Basow, S. A., 32, 46
Bassett, E., 10, 27
Becker, H. S., 81, 96
Berk, L. E., 44, 46
Berndt, T., 33, 46
Berridge, D., 15, 28
Bidell, T. R., 7, 16, 26, 27
Block, J. H., 32, 46
Bloom, P., 83, 96
Body parts, knowledge of, 12–14
Body proportion effect, 10
Bolduc, D., 32, 47
Boston, Massachusetts, 35, 68
Botvin, G. J., 33, 46
Boundaries, 11, 14
Boyatzis, C. J., 5, 12, 15, 27, 31, 35, 46, 50, 52, 58, 60, 62
Boyette, N., 31, 43, 47
Boys, drawings and conversations of, 35–39. See also Gender
Bridson, A., 15, 27
Brown, E. V., 10, 27

Calvin and Hobbes (Watterson), 31
Carothers, T., 83, 96

Cephalocaudal drawing sequences, 10
Change, 85–86
Chapman, L. C, 6, 27
Children Are Artists (Mendolowitz), 84
Children's art. See Drawing, by girls in adolescence; Drawing, children's
Cochran's Q analysis, 69–70, 74
Cocking, R. R., 7, 27
Cohen-Shalev, A., 82, 97
Color, 17, 20
Conformity, 33
Connolly, K., 65, 79
Consensual assessment technique, 51–52
Constructive web, 26
Conversation: components of children's, 33–34; and drawing, of boys, 35–39; and drawing, of girls, 39–43
Copple, C. E., 7, 27
Core dilemma, style as, 82
Cossette, L., 32, 47
Cox, M. V., 5, 10, 11, 12, 15, 20, 22, 26, 27, 31, 32, 43, 46, 65, 79
Criticism, peer, 33. See also Peer collaboration; Peer groups
Cromer, C. C., 33, 46
Culturist's stance, 84–85
Cunningham, A., 33, 34, 44, 46

D'Andrea, M. D., 33, 46
Darwin, C., 26
Davis, J., 83, 97
Dawes, L., 84, 97
Developmental sequences, 52–53
Di Leo, J. H., 9, 27, 79
Differentiation, increasing, 11–14, 20, 24
Distinctiveness, 51. See also Style: components of distinctive
Dramatists, patterners versus, 85
Draw and label strategy, 8, 24
Drawing, by girls in adolescence (case study): comparison of accuracy scores of judges across four time intervals in, 76; continuity of style in, 65–79; correlation between characteristics of, and judges accuracy, 77; method, artists, and judges for, 68–69; overview of, 65–68; presence of distinctive style in, 77–79; procedure for, 69–74; results of, 75–77

99

Drawing, children's: development of individual styles in, 49–62; and drawing and conversations of girls, 39–43; and drawings and conversations of boys, 35–39; gender differences in, 32–33; naturalistic observation of, 31–46
Duncum, P., 44, 46, 83, 97
Duran, R. T., 34, 45, 47

Eades, J., 31, 46, 50, 52, 58, 60, 62
Edelstein, W., 31, 47
Eliefja, C. C., 51, 60–61, 62, 65, 79, 80, 86, 88, 89, 97
Ellis, S., 33, 46
Emotions, conveyance of, 21
Eng, H., 5, 27
Etaugh, C., 33, 47
Evaluation, 34, 45
Events, drawings depicting, 93
Evolution, 26
Expertise, 34, 39, 41, 45
Expression, 65. See also Meaning: intended

Falck, J., 50, 51, 53, 62
Fein, S., 5, 27
Feinburg, S. G., 5, 6, 27, 31, 32, 43, 44, 47
Fenson, L., 5, 6, 19, 20, 27
Ferrara, N., 33, 47
Fischer, K. W., 7, 15, 16, 26, 27, 28
Flannery, K. A., 61, 62
Form, 50, 65
Fortes, M., 65, 79
Freeman, N. H., 5, 6, 9, 9–10, 10, 12, 14, 27

Gandini, L., 51, 62
Gardner, H., 5, 6, 7, 8, 10, 14, 27, 34, 41, 44, 47, 49, 53, 62, 65, 79, 80, 83, 85, 87, 96, 97
Gauvain, M., 6–7, 28, 33, 34, 45, 47
Gender: and drawings and conversations of boys, 35–39; and drawings and conversations of girls, 39–43; and gender segregation, 33; sources of difference in, 32–33
Generic prototypes, 17
Gestural components, 16–19
Girls: drawing by, in adolescence (case study), 65–79; drawings and conversations of, 39–43. See also Gender

Goldsmith, L. T., 5, 6, 28
Golomb, C., 5, 6, 10, 12, 14, 28, 85, 97
Gombrich, E. H., 53, 62, 82, 97
Goodman, N., 83
Goodmanian aesthetics, 83
Goodnow, J., 5, 11, 12, 14, 17, 28, 84, 97
Graphic realism, 34, 44, 53
Gridley, P. F., 11, 28

Harris, D., 65, 79
Hartley, J. L., 51, 60–61, 62, 65, 79, 80, 86, 87, 88, 89, 97
Harvard University, 83
Hennessey, B. A., 51–52, 60, 62
Homa, D., 65, 79

Inanimate drawings, 93
Inhelder, B., 11, 12, 28
Intent, aesthetic, 49
Intention, 83; and aesthetic intent, 49; and intentional representation, 8
Intentional representation, 8
Internal modal, 14

Jacklin, C. N., 33, 47
Jackowitz, E. R., 50, 62
Jacobs, C., 15, 27
Jarvis, 12
Jensen, D.V.C., 51, 60–61, 62, 65, 79, 80, 86, 87, 88, 89, 97

Kaplan, B., 7, 11, 16–17, 25–26, 28, 29
Karmiloff-Smith, A., 12, 16, 28, 34, 44, 47, 79, 80
Kawecki, I., 32, 47
Kellogg, R., 5, 8, 14, 28, 49, 62
Kitchener, K. S., 15, 28
Koff, E., 16, 65, 68, 78, 79
Kohlmann, R., 11, 28
Korzenik, D., 6, 28

Laible, D. J., 16, 65
Lange-Küttner, C., 31, 47
Lark-Horowitz, B., 32–33, 47
Lavan, S. K., 15, 27
Lewis, C., 15, 28
Lewis, H. P., 32–33, 47
Liben, L., 11, 28
Light, P., 15, 28
Likert scale, 69
Lindstrom, M., 89, 97
Liss, M. B., 33, 47

Longitudinal case study: background to, 5; conclusions drawn from, 24–27; and drawing in the zone of proximal development, 14–16; and early drawings, 8–11; and increasing differentiation in drawings, 11–14; and instance of microgenesis, 19–24; method for, 7–24; overview of, 6–7; and personal meaning and problem solving in drawings, 16–19; subject, setting, and procedure for, 7–24; symbolic and social processes in, 5–27
Luca, M., 32–33, 47
Luria, Z., 33, 48
Lyle, E., 12, 15, 27

Maccoby, E. E., 33, 47
Machotka, P., 44, 47
Machover, K., 31, 47
Malcuit, G., 32, 47
Matlew, M., 65, 79
McEwen, F., 15, 28
McNiff, K., 31, 43, 47
Meaning: intended, 50; personal, 16–19
Meaning, personal, in drawing, 16–19
Menarche, 78
Mendelson, M. J., 7, 28
Mendolowitz, D. M., 84, 85, 87, 97
Michaelson, P., 12, 15, 27
Microgenesis, 19–24
Middle childhood, 33, 53, 61
Milbrath, C., 84, 93, 97
Mind in Society (Vygotsky), 45
Murray, F. B., 33, 46

Neutralist's stance, 83; versus culturalist's stance, 84–85
Nomothetic approach, 5
Norm, conflation of, with form, 82

Observational learning, 33
O'Keeffe, G., 39–40
One-way analyses of variance (ANOVAs), 58–59
Ongoing commentary, 40
Organization, increasing, 20
Orthogenetic principle, 24, 25–26
Other, representation of, 17
Overlapping rule, 11, 14

Parisella, J., 31, 46, 60, 62
Parker, L., 50, 51, 53, 62
Parkin, C., 5, 26, 27

Parsons, M. J., 81, 96, 97
Participation, guided, 34. See also Peer collaboration
Patterners, versus dramatists, 85
Peer collaboration: fifth-grade class case study of, 35–43; and guided participation, 34; processes in, 33–34; quality of communication in, 44–45
Peer groups: gender issues related to, 33; and peer criticism, 33
Perner, J., 11, 28
Perpendicularity, 11
Perry, M. D., 15, 26, 29
Persistence, 85–86
Personal style, Mendolowitz's definition of, 85
Perspective, use of, 67
Pesonen, T., 7–8, 50, 68, 81, 86, 90, 93, 97
Piaget, J., 11, 12, 28
Play, symbolic object use in, 50
Pomerleau, A., 32, 47
Powlishta, K. K., 33, 47
Problem solving, in drawing, 16–19, 53
Project Zero (Harvard University), 83
Proportionality, 12–14, 20
Prospective analysis, 86–90
Proximal development, zone of (Vygotsky), 7, 14–16
Pufall, P. B., 7–8, 50, 51, 53, 62, 68, 81, 86, 90, 93, 96, 97

Quality, aesthetic, 49

Radziszewska, B., 34, 45, 47
Realism, graphic, 34, 44
Reeves, J. B., 31, 43, 47
Refinement, 96
Repertoire, 26
Representation: of other, 17; and representational art, 5, 8
Retrospective analysis, 90–93
Rierdan, J., 78, 79
Robinson, E. J., 15, 29
RoboCop characters, 35–37
Rogoff, B., 33, 34, 45, 46, 47
Roman, K., 65, 79
Rosenblatt, E., 65, 79, 80
Rothschild, L., 84, 87, 97
Rubenstein, J., 31, 43, 47
Rubin, C., 31, 43, 47
Rules, drawing, 20
Russell, C., 15, 28

Schirrmacher, R., 7, 28
Schwartz, S. N., 49, 78, 80
Self-consciousness, 33, 37, 41
Self-criticism, 39
Selfe, L, 5, 9, 28
Serial order effect, 10
Siegler, R. S., 25, 28, 53, 62
Silverstone, E., 68, 78, 79
Size, relative, 9
Skill, developmental range of (Fischer and Bidell), 7, 26
Smith, A., 7, 27
Smith, N. R., 5, 6, 8, 28, 50, 62
Socialization: artistic, 6; and gender differences, 32–33; and image of artistic development as socially embedded, 45
Somerville, S. C., 32, 39, 47, 50, 51, 60–61, 62, 65, 77, 79, 80, 86, 87, 88, 89, 97
Stages, presumption of, 25
Style: case study in, 54–57; components of distinctive, 59–60; and components used and ratings for twelve children with distinctive styles, 61; consensual assessment technique for determining distinctive, 51–52; as core dilemma, 82; definition of, 50; definition of distinctive, 51; development of artistic, in children's artworld, 81–96; and developmental sequences, 52–53; emergence of distinctive, 58–59; identifying components of, 50–51; local norms of, 33; and personal style, 85; restructured, versus refinement, 96; Wölfflin model of, 82
Subject matter, 50, 65
Symbolic development, focus on, 6
Symbolic flexibility, range of, 15
Tadpole person, 8, 9, 24, 25

Teasley, S. D., 34, 44, 45, 47
Technical guidance, 45
Theme: personal exploration of, in artworld, 85; and style in children's artworld, 93–95; and thematic preferences, 43; three categories of, 93
Thomas, G. V., 9–10, 15, 28, 29
Thorne, B., 32, 33, 47, 48
Training, art, 53
Tsalimi, A., 9–10, 28
Tudge, J.R.H., 45, 48
Tukey post hoc analyses, 59
Twain, M., 26

Van Sommers, P., 14, 28, 53, 62
Verbalization, 7, 44
Verticality, 11
Vinter, A., 7, 9, 28, 80
Von Cziesch Jensen, D., 86, 87, 88, 89, 97
Vygotsky, L. S., 7, 15, 26, 29, 34, 45, 48

Watson, M. W., 16, 49, 50, 61, 62, 65, 78, 80
Watterson, W., 31
Werner, H., 7, 11, 16–17, 29
Whitin, R., 93, 97
Wieder, C. G., 49, 62
Wilkins, P., 84, 97
Wilson, B., 83, 84, 97
Wimmer, H., 11, 28
Winner, E., 8, 12, 29, 65, 78, 79, 80, 83, 85, 93, 97
Wolf, D. P., 7, 15, 16–17, 25, 26, 27, 29
Wölfflin, H., 82, 83

Zhi, Z., 15, 29
Zimmerman, E, 5, 6, 29

Back Issue/Subscription Order Form

Copy or detach and send to:
Jossey-Bass, 350 Sansome Street, San Francisco, CA 94104-1342

Call or fax toll free!
Phone 888-378-2537 6AM–5PM PST; Fax 800-605-2665

Back issues:	Please send me the following issues at $25 each (Important: please include series initials and issue number, such as CD88)

1. CD _____

_____

_____

$ _____ Total for single issues

$ _____ Shipping charges (for single issues *only;* subscriptions are exempt from shipping charges): Up to $30, add $5^{50} • $30^{01}–$50, add $6^{50} $50^{01}–$75, add $8 • $75^{01}–$100, add $10 • $100^{01}–$150, add $12 Over $150, call for shipping charge

Subscriptions   Please ❏ start   ❏ renew my subscription to *New Directions for Child and Adolescent Development* for the year _____ at the following rate:

U.S.:	❏ Individual $68	❏ Institutional $125
Canada:	❏ Individual $68	❏ Institutional $165
All others:	❏ Individual $92	❏ Institutional $199

NOTE: Subscriptions are quarterly, and are for the calendar year only. Subscriptions begin with the Spring issue of the year indicated above.

$ _____ Total single issues and subscriptions (Add appropriate sales tax for your state for single issues. No sales tax on U.S. subscriptions. Canadian residents add GST for subscriptions and single issues.)

❏ Payment enclosed (U.S. check or money order only)

❏ VISA, MC, AmEx, Discover Card #_____ Exp. date_____

Signature _____ Day phone _____

❏ Bill me (U.S. institutional orders only. Purchase order required)

Purchase order #_____

Federal Tax ID 135593032 GST 89102-8502

Name _____

Address _____

_____

Phone_____ E-mail _____

For more information about Jossey-Bass, visit our Web site at:
www.josseybass.com   **PRIORITY CODE = ND1**

OTHER TITLES AVAILABLE IN THE NEW DIRECTIONS FOR CHILD AND
ADOLESCENT DEVELOPMENT SERIES
William Damon, Editor-in-Chief

CD89 Rights and Wrongs: How Children and Young Adults Evaluate the World, *Marta Laupa*
CD88 Recent Advances in the Measurement of Acceptance and Rejection in the Peer System, *Antonius H. N. Cillessen, William M. Bukowski*
CD87 Variability in the Social Construction of the Child, *Sara Harkness, Catherine Raeff, Charles M. Super*
CD86 Conflict as a Context for Understanding Maternal Beliefs About Child Rearing and Children's Misbehavior, *Paul D. Hastings, Caroline C. Piotrowski*
CD85 Homeless and Working Youth Around the World: Exploring Developmental Issues, *Marcela Raffaelli, Reed W. Larson*
CD84 The Role of Peer Groups in Adolescent Social Identity: Exploring the Importance of Stability and Change, *Jeffrey A. McLellan, Mary Jo V. Pugh*
CD83 Development and Cultural Change: Reciprocal Processes, *Elliot Turiel*
CD82 Temporal Rhythms in Adolescence: Clocks, Calendars, and the Coordination of Daily Life, *Ann C. Crouter, Reed W. Larson*
CD81 Socioemotional Development Across Cultures, *Dinesh Sharma, Kurt W. Fischer*
CD80 Sociometry Then and Now: Building on Six Decades of Measuring Children's Experiences with the Peer Group, *William M. Bukowski, Antonius H. Cillessen*
CD79 The Nature and Functions of Gesture in Children's Communication, *Jana M. Iverson, Susan Goldin-Meadow*
CD78 Romantic Relationships in Adolescence: Developmental Perspectives, *Shmuel Shulman, W. Andrew Collins*
CD77 The Communication of Emotion: Current Research from Diverse Perspectives, *Karen Caplovitz Barrett*
CD76 Culture as a Context for Moral Development, *Herbert D. Saltzstein*
CD75 The Emergence of Core Domains of Thought: Children's Reasoning About Physical, Psychological, and Biological Phenomena, *Henry M. Wellman, Kayoko Inagaki*
CD74 Understanding How Family-Level Dynamics Affect Children's Development: Studies of Two-Parent Families, *James P. McHale, Philip A. Cowan*
CD73 Children's Autonomy, Social Competence, and Interactions with Adults and Other Children: Exploring Connections and Consequences, *Melanie Killen*
CD72 Creativity from Childhood Through Adulthood: The Developmental Issues, *Mark A. Runco*
CD71 Leaving Home: Understanding the Transition to Adulthood, *Julia A. Graber, Judith Semon Dubas*
CD69 Exploring Young Children's Concepts of Self and Other Through Conversation, *Linda L. Sperry, Patricia A. Smiley*
CD68 African American Family Life: Its Structural and Ecological Aspects, *Melvin N. Wilson*
CD67 Cultural Practices as Contexts for Development, *Jacqueline J. Goodnow, Peggy J. Miller, Frank Kessel*
CD65 Childhood Gender Segregation: Causes and Consequences, *Campbell Leaper*
CD64 Children, Youth, and Suicide: Developmental Perspectives, *Gil G. Noam, Sophie Borst*
CD59 The Role of Play in the Development of Thought, *Marc H. Bornstein, Anne Watson O'Reilly*
CD52 Religious Development in Childhood and Adolescence, *Fritz K. Oser, W. George Scarlett*